There Came a
Sound
from Heaven

There Came a Sound from Heaven

The Life Story
of
DR. ED DUFRESNE

Written by
Nancy Dufresne

The story of a life filled with sounds from heaven

This book has been written in honor of Ed Dufresne's thirty-fifth year of ministry, celebrated in the year 2000. Although he didn't know it was being written, we thought the recording of God's dealings in his life to be beneficial to the body of Christ so that all could see the strong hand of God that rests upon the life of any person who will "only believe."

Endorsements

Jeanne and I have been friends with Ed Dufresne for 25 of his 35 years of ministry. We have watched each other's children grow up . . . and now our grandchildren.

In the early years of our ministries the Lord spoke to me about the anointing on Ed's life and ministry. He called my attention to the words of the Apostle Paul in I Corinthians 2:4, *"And His speech and preaching will not be with enticing words of man's wisdom but in demonstration of the Spirit and of Power."*

Over the years, when we have ministered together, I have seen this come to pass many times. We send our love, prayers, and congratulations to a man of God, for thirty-five years of service.

Pastor Happy & Jeanne Caldwell
Little Rock, AR

Any time one has the opportunity and privilege to know the details of a life filled with faith, they should take it, especially if that person has been used and mightily anointed by God. Ed Dufresne has walked with Jesus and has been witness to the greatness of God.

I know Gloria and I have been personal witnesses of his life and ministry. What God has done for one, He'll do for another if they will do the things that it takes to develop a covenant relationship with Jesus. Ed has done that. Find out what he did, and you can do it too, especially in the area of commitment to God's Word and a non-compromising life of faith.

I want to thank Nancy for making Ed's story available to us, not only to enjoy, but to inspire us all to continue to reach for God's best.

JESUS IS LORD
Kenneth Copeland
Ft. Worth, TX

I have had the privilege of knowing Dr. Ed Dufresne for many years and one thing that always stands clear in my mind is that this man of God is full of integrity and can be trusted in the Body of Christ. He moves with such power and love in ministering to people. When you go to a meeting where Dr. Ed Dufresne is, you will never be disappointed, you will have a fresh touch of heaven every time. This man of God seeks God for people's lives. I know that most people call Dr. Ed Dufresne a prophet, but I have never heard him declare himself a prophet. He truly is a prophet and man of God that I love and respect, and I know the Body of Christ does around the world.

In a meeting he prophesied to me on a specific gift that was coming my way. That specific gift came in exactly like he said two weeks later, and it was pure Holy Ghost.

The power of God moves through this man and I am just one of countless thousands that has been touched by this man and his ministry I consider it a great honor and privilege to know this man of God. He truly is a breath of fresh air, desperately treasured and needed today.

Mac Gober
Autaugaville, AL

I have known Ed Dufresne over 20 years. I remember when Buddy, my late husband, and I first met Ed at Crenshaw Christian Center. We became good covenant friends and over the years I have appreciated the tenacity with which he pursues the things of God.

Ed has always been hungry for God and willing to do whatever it took to be obedient, spending hours in prayer and preparation so that he could bring a word fresh from heaven to encourage the people. He is a man of integrity, one who will do what he says. I believe he is a true prophet of God.

May his testimony and life story encourage you to hunger after God and seek Him with all your heart.

Reverend Pat Harrison
Tulsa, OK

My father, Dr. Lester Sumrall, declared that the last great revival before the Lord's return would be characterized by a supernatural demonstration of God's power through the gifts of the Holy Spirit.

Like few other, Ed Dufresne's life and legacy of faith have been marked by an undeniable manifestation of Holy Spirit miracles, signs and wonders.

Today, there seem to be so many seeking the power of God without having the passion it takes to stay in the race, fight the good fight, and pay the price. One thing that we have witnessed over the years is that Ed Dufresne is a man of uncompromising integrity and tenacity towards the Word of God. He's taken "the Doctor's" words to heart and put them into practice . . . "Live Right and Don't Quit!"

Ed, we believe your next 35 years will be even greater!

Pastor Stephen Sumrall
South Bend, IN

A believer's life is always influenced and often defined by those who have spoken into it. For those in ministry, a faithful friend is one who — by his presence, his word, and his manner of life — takes another to a higher degree of faith in God. In my own life, such a man and such a friend is Dr. Ed Dufresne.

Hebrews 13:7-8 says, *"Remember them which have the rule over you, who have spoken unto you the word of God: whose faith follow, considering the end of their conversation. Jesus Christ the same yesterday, and today, and forever."*

Having known the faith of Ed Dufresne, I have had the privilege of receiving from the depth of his walk with God. The influence and impartation Dr. Dufresne received from his mentors lives and burns within him, and from his heart he imparts that same measure of intensity of faith in God.

His life is a demonstration of the faithfulness of God and of the integrity of the Word.

Ed Dufresne can be characterized simply as "a man of the Spirit," who really believes that Jesus Christ is the same, yesterday, today, and forever. I am truly blessed to have received so richly from the ministry and friendship of Dr. Ed Dufresne.

Pastor Scott Webb
Birmingham, AL

Dedication

No man travels alone in his walk with God, for he carries with him the impartations of God-filled men who fathered and trained him in the faith.

With deepest love, honor, and gratitude, this book is dedicated to three men who have, in different ways, shared in the shaping of Ed Dufresne's spiritual life.

The place a father holds in the heart of his son is unequalled by anyone – spiritually, this truth runs even deeper. Such is the place that Kenneth E. Hagin, Sr. holds in the life of Ed Dufresne. Through his faith, his walk of love, his ministry and private conversations, Brother Hagin has been that fatherly voice in the life and ministry of Ed Dufresne, bringing fatherly insight, stability, and guidance. We're so thankful we can affectionately call him "Dad."

To Dr. Lester Sumrall, although he has now gone home to be with the Lord, he still speaks through the life of Ed Dufresne, who sat under his ever-watchful, parental eye and pastoral care. We still hold fast to the spirit of faith and boldness we caught from this general of God.

To Kenneth Copeland, who was the first to preach God's Word to a young Ed Dufresne with a fire that continues to burn in our lives and keeps us ever mindful of our all-conquering covenant.

To our ever-loving heavenly Father, and to our matchless Redeemer who paid the ultimate price – it's all to Your glory.

Acknowledgements

A project like this never becomes a reality without the hands and hearts of many people who catch the vision.

To Sandy Ollen, who wholeheartedly jumped into this project, and quickly placed in our hands hundreds of pages of typed sermons, manuscripts, and resource materials. We wouldn't have wanted to do it without you!

To Sharon Morgan, Francine LaRue, Stephanie Lively, and Mark Franco, who helped to gather materials and prepare the manuscript. Thank you for running with us to complete this labor of love.

To Mark Turner, who opened the avenue of completion and out of his love and respect for this man and his ministry, encouraged us to place the life story of Ed Dufresne into the hands of the body of Christ.

To Jim McKenna of Sumrall Publishing, who welcomed the opportunity to publish the story of God's dealings with His man.

Thank you for loving the man, honoring the ministry, and helping us fulfill that which God placed in our hearts.

Contents

Foreword

This book is written, not to man's glory, but to God's glory, who takes men, in spite of human failures, faults, and short-comings, puts His own life into their beings, empowers them with His holy anointing, then sends them forth to lead and to serve, blessing humanity.

In the life of Moses we see an experience, an event, that forever marked the lives of those looking on:

And it came to pass, as Moses entered into the tabernacle, the cloudy pillar descended, and stood at the door of the tabernacle, and the Lord talked with Moses.

And all the people saw the cloudy pillar stand at the tabernacle door: and all the people rose up and worshipped, every man in his tent door.

And the Lord spake unto Moses face to face, as a man speaketh unto his friend. And he turned again into the camp: but his servant Joshua, the son of Nun, a young man, departed not out of the tabernacle.

Exodus 33:9-11

All of God's people looked upon the place where God descended to visit with one man and the presence of God caused them all to stand at the door of their own dwellings and worship God. Only one man had the experience, but all saw the God who visited with him and worship to God was the result.

Likewise, can we not look into the experiences in the life of a man visited by God and rise up in our dwelling places and our homes, and begin to worship the God who not only visits with man, but puts His own life and Spirit within him?

Yes, the experiences and encounters with God recorded in this book are those of one man, but all who wish to look upon these occurrences can freely see God and have their own lives marked by this God who still visits and indwells men. When God visits with a man, many will rise and worship God. Through the experiences of other men, we can see God.

Joshua, being Moses' servant, was permitted to follow Moses into the tent. Although he followed Moses in, he didn't follow him out. His heart was following his God, not a man. Joshua lingered in the aftereffects of another man's experience and it caused him to worship God and draw nearer to Him.

May we too, through the pages of this book, follow a man into his own experiences with God. But then let us also linger in the aftereffects and visit with God, worshipping Him and drawing nearer to Him. Let us hear for ourselves *the sounds that come from heaven.*

Nancy Dufresne

Part I
His Life and Ministry

Chapter 1

In the Beginning . . .

How do we glimpse with clarity into the life of any man without visiting the lives of those who surrounded his early years?

Although Ed Dufresne was born June 10, 1941, in Long Beach, California, the hand of God was intervening in his life long before that day. His mother, Norma Emma Schwengel, was born on August 30, 1924, to Elmer and Florence Schwengel in Philadelphia, Pennsylvania, and was of German descent. Little is known about her parents and family, but true to her German bloodline, she grew to be a strong-willed, quick-tempered brunette who had many capabilities.

She was quite young when she met the handsome Edward F. Dufresne, who was also born in Philadelphia, Pennsylvania, on September 13, 1923. It wasn't long until the young couple found themselves in love.

Their courtship began prior to the outbreak of World War II and the romance between the two was flourishing. They, no doubt, thought they had much time to grow together and to let their relationship develop, but little did they know that Edward Dufresne was soon to enter the American war ranks. With the realization that they were soon to be separated, their future became cloudy and those prewar days were suddenly darkened by uncertainty, questions, and unrest.

It was during these uneasy days that their relationship was to face an additional hardship. Norma learned that she was pregnant. Marriage had been seriously discussed by the young couple, but had not been firmly decided upon. To be pregnant and unwed was a situation of shame and embarrassment for them and they were afraid to tell their families, knowing their reactions would be less than supportive.

What should they do? This was the question with which the young couple battled. Since Edward was to join the Navy, neither one of them was sure of the days ahead. They spent many long hours trying to decide how they would handle their future. They didn't want to be forced into a marriage and the war had made their future too uncertain.

Their decision? They decided that Norma would go to a backyard abortionist and abort the baby. This way they wouldn't have to tell their families of their inappropriate relationship and would spare the families the embarrassment of an untimely pregnancy.

It is at this point that we must jump ahead in the story forty-four years to see the intervening hand of God. The year is 1984 and the location is Munich, Germany, the homeland of Norma's ancestors.

Angels in the Building

Ed Dufresne is standing on the platform of a church during his nine-day European preaching tour. It was a night to be remembered, marked by the miraculous and God's supernatural power.

The service had begun with Ed preaching about how to receive the healing power of God. The anointing had charged the atmosphere and the German congregation was hungrily taking in every word. Right in the middle of Ed's sermon, there was a disturbance and a cry from the back of the church building.

"I'm going to take my healing now! I've waited thirty years for this and tonight is my night!" Up the aisle came an elderly man, stooped over at the waist, telling his story as he approached the front.

"I'm a preacher! But thirty years ago I was arrested for preaching and was thrown into a German labor camp. My job for all these years has been to carry firewood; that's why I can't straighten up my back. But tonight is my night!"

Without anyone laying a hand on the elderly man, he slowly began to straighten right before everyone's eyes. Taller and taller he rose until he was standing perfectly erect — but he didn't stop there! As he rose to his full height, he kept rising! An unseen force had gripped the back of his neck, pulled up the stooped figure, and continued to hold him, lifting him completely off the ground until his feet dangled in midair with the tips of his toes barely brushing the floor.

Everyone's eyes opened wide as they saw this elderly saint, moved on by God's healing power.

The congregation saw the man's body straightened and then held dangling in midair, but Ed saw an angel behind the man, pulling him to an erect position and then continuing to lift him in midair as his twisted body was made whole.

Miracles Breed Miracles

In the Word we see time and time again that miracles breed miracles. One supernatural act provokes another supernatural act.

It was into this miracle that another supernatural encounter with God occurred and a hidden puzzle piece from the past of Ed Dufresne's life was brought into view.

Since Ed's family on his mother's side was of German descent, it seems to be quite fitting that God chose to reveal some of his family history to him while on German soil.

In the Spirit, God took Ed through some of the events of his childhood, showing him His hand of protection on his life. God began this visitation by saying, "When your mother found out that she was pregnant with you, which was before your parents were married, they decided to go to a back alley abortionist to abort you, but I sent an angel to stop that from happening and to lead them to marry, sparing your life."

Ed did know that his mother became pregnant with him while she was yet unwed, but, of course, they had never mentioned their plans of abortion to anyone.

Hanging from the Bridge

God proceeded to show him another event of his past where His hand had been upon his life to protect it. God reminded Ed of the time when he was twelve years old and

6

was riding in a vehicle with his dad. His dad was drunk and had a wreck on a bridge. The vehicle hung dangerously off the edge of the bridge, tottering back and forth. God said, "I sent an angel that night to keep that vehicle from falling off the edge of the bridge."

Ed remembered the incident well. His dad drank heavily and this particular night, as his dad was driving them home, he fell asleep. Ed was in the passenger's side, terrified as he felt the vehicle bounce from one side of the bridge to the other, break through the wall, then totter over the edge. It could easily have fallen over the edge if any weight in the truck had shifted. In near hysterics, Ed trembled violently, not knowing what to do.

Suddenly, the nose of the truck lifted up and fell back onto the road. Ed had no idea how that had happened, but being so terror-stricken, he didn't take the time to figure it out. Days after the incident, Ed was still shaking — so terrifying was the experience.

But now, while in Germany and with God revealing to him His own intervening hand, he knew that angels had rescued him and his dad that night.

We won't ever know until we get to heaven the number of times God has intervened to spare the lives of His children.

God watches over us with His tender care, and if we'll follow the leading of our spirit, He'll always lead us away from tragedy if we'll take the time to get quiet before Him and hear what He has to say.

Although neither Ed nor his dad were born again when

this incident occurred, Psalm 145:8,9 tells us, *"The Lord is gracious, and full of compassion; slow to anger, and of great mercy. The Lord is good to ALL: and his tender mercies are over all his works."*

God is good to *all!* That would certainly include those who are lost and without God. It was God's goodness and mercy that caused Him to intervene in the life of a terrified little boy and a drunken father. It's by His mercy and grace their lives were spared that night, and as God reminded Ed of this incident during that service in Germany, Ed was blessed to see the caring hand of God in his life.

Yes, It's True

When Ed returned from Germany, he had an opportunity to talk with his dad. "When you found out Mom was pregnant with me before you were married, did you plan to go to a back alley abortionist to abort me?" Ed questioned.

With a look of shame and tear-filled eyes came the confirmation, "Yes, son, we were. But since I was raised Catholic, I knew that it was wrong and I couldn't go through with it."

Little did that young couple know that heaven's ministering spirits were active in their lives to cause the plan and will of God to come to pass, which meant sparing the life of their unborn baby.

How great is the love and mercy of God toward us!

> *For You did form my inward parts; You did knit me together in my mother's womb.*
>
> *I will confess and praise You for You are fearful and wonderful and for the awful wonder of my birth! Wonderful are Your works, and that my inner self knows right well.*

My frame was not hidden from You when I was being formed in secret [and] intricately and curiously wrought [as if embroidered with various colors] in the depths of the earth [a region of darkness and mystery].

Your eyes saw my unformed substance, and in Your book all the days [of my life] were written before ever they took shape, when as yet there was none of them.

How precious and weighty also are Your thoughts to me, O God! How vast is the sum of them!

Psalm 139:13-17 AMP

With heaven's intervention, this young couple abandoned their thoughts of abortion and eloped to Tecate, Mexico, since Norma was only fifteen at the time and didn't have parental consent for marriage.

Satan, the Destroyer

The devil still continued trying to destroy, for when Norma Dufresne gave birth to her new son, she received improper medical care. The afterbirth was not removed upon delivery and her whole system became poisoned, causing her to linger at the brink of death, but God's mercy was apparent again, and she recovered to health.

Since Ed's parents and relatives were not born again, the home he grew up in was void of any godly influences and was full of all kinds of problems.

Prior to their marriage, when Norma's father found out that she was pregnant with Ed, the embarrassment and shame were more than he could handle, so he committed suicide leaving behind a note implying that his daughter's pregnancy was the reason for his actions.

For a girl at the close of her teen years to be burdened with the fault of her father's suicide was more than she could bear.

There was alcoholism on both sides of their families, so the newlyweds vowed they would never drink alcoholic beverages, for they didn't want their new home together to mirror the homes they were raised in. Although intentions were good, without God in their lives, their good intentions fell by the wayside and social drinking crept into Edward and Norma's lives, which later escalated to alcoholism for both of them.

For Norma, the drinking became a way of escape from the blame that fell on her for her father's death, but eventually her mind broke down under the guilt. Time and again she was placed in the mental ward of the hospital. It was this kind of environment that Ed and his four siblings grew up in.

Marital problems and breakups were commonplace, and to make matters worse, Ed was left, as a little boy, to help tend and care for his baby brothers and sisters when his mother was unable to cope.

Those without Jesus are without hope, peace, love, and light. What heartbreaking home settings this creates for children.

Mama, Please Forgive Me

Norma was continuously blamed by family members for the unsettled state of the home, which only served to add more heartbreak to her life. Not knowing Jesus and not knowing to cast her cares on the Lord, she lived a life full of darkness.

All of Ed's life he had heard his mother blamed as being

the reason for all the problems at home. As a result, he grew up with a hatred toward his mother. It became easy to lay all the blame on her for their problems, so Ed blamed her as well.

But after Ed was born again, God began dealing with him about his attitude toward her. Ed found out that Satan is the destroyer, and that he was the one behind all their heartache.

God taught him that if he was to be blessed, he had to honor his mother and his father regardless of their faults and failures. Ed went to his mother and repented to her for how he had treated her through the years and asked for her forgiveness.

It Was a Home Run

It was at the age of forty-five that Norma's darkness ended. She had just come off a drinking binge and had called Ed, who was born again by this time. As he had many times before, he talked to her about making Jesus the Lord of her life, but this time she didn't refuse; she received Jesus into her heart. It was a thrill and a joy for Ed to be able to lead his own mother to Christ.

After Norma prayed with him, she went into her bedroom and laid down on the bed. When morning dawned, Norma was found dead. She had gone home to be with the Lord.

Ed was shocked by her death and questioned God as to why she had died, seeing that she had just given her life to Jesus. Ed had looked forward to developing and enjoying a relationship with his mom that he had never experienced.

God answered Ed, "Son, her mind was so broken down

and she had destroyed her body through years of abuse. She was unable to believe Me for her restoration. She was right with Me for the first time in her life; so in My mercy, I allowed her to come on home to be with Me." How Ed rejoiced at the goodness of God!

Someone made the statement to Ed regarding his mother's salvation, "Well, she just barely slid into heaven."

"Yes," rejoiced Ed, " but it was a home run!"

The mercy of God is astounding!

In several visions that Ed has had, his mother was standing at Jesus' side. "She doesn't even look like the same person. She looks so beautiful and happy now," he would remark each time he was allowed to see her.

What a comfort it is to know that those loved ones who have gone home to be with Jesus are ever rejoicing, ever happy, ever youthful, ever strong, ever healthy and ever peaceful. Therefore, we rejoice in God's goodness.

Chapter 2
Don't Give Up on Your Family!

The story for Ed's dad, Edward Dufresne, Sr., is also one that included a life of alcoholism. Although he lived to be seventy-one, he almost died several times. When Ed would talk to him about giving his life to Jesus, he continually declined. Every time his dad was hospitalized, he always warned the family members, "Don't tell little Eddie." He didn't want Ed to talk to him about being born again.

No one had to tell Ed when his dad was hospitalized, God always told him; and invariably, Ed would show up at the hospital asking his dad to pray with him.

It was on one such occasion that God told Ed his dad was again in the hospital dying. Ed showed up at his bedside and said "Dad, it's time for you to give your heart to Jesus."

"I want a priest," his dad requested.

"I'm your priest, Dad!"

Finally, he prayed the sinner's prayer with Ed.

God, Give Him Two More Years

The doctors had only given him hours to live, but since his dad just got saved, Ed made a request of God. "My dad and I have never been close, so I'm asking You to give me two more years with him so we can have fellowship that we've never had before."

God granted Ed's request. His dad recovered and lived another two years and twenty nine days, then went home to be with the Lord.

Since that time, God has also allowed Ed to see his dad in a vision standing with Jesus, just as he has seen his mother. What comfort this has brought to Ed to know that his dad and mother are experiencing a peace and joy they never experienced while on this earth.

Stand on Your Covenant

Ed has always taken a bold stand on God's Word on behalf of his family, saying, "God, Your Word says that if I believe on the Lord Jesus Christ that I shall be saved *and my house*" (Acts 16:31). This is my covenant with You and I say that not one of my family members will die and go to hell, but they will all be born again and will go to heaven." God has proven Himself to be true to His Word and Ed has not only seen the salvation of his parents, but of other family members as well.

Never give up on your family. Keep surrounding them with faith and love. Stand on the firm foundation of your covenant with God, for God's Word cannot fail!

The Man Who Wouldn't Quit

George Mueller, who was a minister in England during the 1800's, tells of an unsaved man who was considered by others to be beyond help. But Brother Mueller refused to give up on him. In George Mueller's journal, it is recorded that he called this man's name before God every day for fifty years claiming his salvation.

George Mueller never lived to see this man's conversion, but the man gave his heart to Christ at George Mueller's funeral.

Never give up!

Chapter 3

The Teenage Years

Ed was raised Catholic, although he and his family weren't very devout; every Easter and Christmas did find them at the local parish, with Ed faithfully putting his dollar in the collection basket.

Occasionally, as a young boy, Ed would visit the priest for confession, but because he didn't know everything he should say, he would make up lies of things he had supposedly done wrong and tell them to the priest.

Boys Will Be Boys

Like every other growing kid, Ed found plenty of mischief with which to occupy himself. Much of his time was spent with his younger brothers, chasing each other through the yard with axes and hatchets. Not really the best pastime for brothers, but an unwholesome environment produces unwholesome activities.

There was also a time, as a young boy, when he helped put debris on a train track which almost derailed a train. He thought he had gotten by with it until some FBI agents showed up on his front porch to see him.

They let him know that his actions put him in jeopardy of going to prison. Only wanting to scare him, the agents successfully accomplished their goal. They gave him a talking to that caused him to walk the straight and narrow for awhile.

When Ed did get into any trouble, he always hoped that his mother wasn't the one who would dole out the punishment. Time and again he would remark, *"That woman would whip you hard enough to leave welts on your behind! It was that German temper she had!*

"When she went to whip me, I'd take off running! I'd run out of the house, and into the field and sleep there all night long, just to get away from her.

"One time I had done something wrong and she grabbed the belt. As usual, I took off running through the house and she was running after me. We had been missing the screen off the back door for a long time. I didn't know it, but she had just put a new screen on that day. With her chasing after me, I headed for the back door and ran right through the new screen door! Boy, did I ever catch it when she caught me!"

Ed found out early that the best way to survive in a home void of happiness and peace was to stay away from it as much as he could. This developed in Ed the ability to survive on his own.

He was already becoming quite an entrepreneur, even at such a young age. He would get hold of all the fixins' to make lemonade, then he'd build a stand out on a nearby corner, and sell the lemonade to all those who happened to pass by. He'd come home with his pockets bulging and feeling mighty proud of himself!

One of his most favorite things to do was to go fishing off the wharf and at the end of the day, sell what he had caught.

Ways to make money were endless for him and he became pretty good at turning a buck.

What Am I, a Puppet?

Although he was raised in a less than devout Catholic home, Ed always had a hunger for God and longed to know Him. It was at the age of twelve that Ed first remembered the dealings of God with his heart.

When God speaks to us, that moment is forever marked in our memory. We can remember where we were, what we were doing, and all the events surrounding that moment — that moment is frozen in time. It was one such moment for this twelve-year-old boy.

While walking down the sidewalk one day, he went to take a step off the curb and as he did, up from his heart rose a cry, "What am I, God? Am I a puppet on a string?"

Into his heart flooded a revelation of God's existence. He knew from that time that God was real and his heart reached out to Him, longing to know Him.

Not knowing how to reach God, to know God, or to walk with Him, Ed's youth was filled with wanderings, searching for meaning to life and looking for something worth living for.

You'll Never Amount to Anything

Although Ed's relationship with his father wasn't a close one, like every other young boy, Ed yearned for his father's approval. As he was growing up, his dad would point up to a location of homes in Palos Verdes and say, "You can never live up there unless you become a doctor, a lawyer, or a gangster! If you don't get an education, you'll never amount to anything!"

How those words stung the growing boy. In his own mind, to have his father's approval he had to get a good education and become someone important. This seemed like an impossibility.

Ed desperately struggled in school amidst a home life of turmoil, but he never finished high school. Without a good education, he could never amount to anything, according to his father; and unless he became someone important he couldn't have his father's approval. This weighed heavily on Ed as he grew up and he became determined to win his dad's affection.

God's Blessings Make Us Rich

Years later, after he was born again and was in full-time ministry, Ed did move to the area his father had pointed out to him as a young boy, known as Palos Verdes, living there for eight years. It wasn't having an advanced education or carrying a doctor or lawyer's title by his name that got him there, but it was because of the blessings of God on his life. *"The blessing of the Lord, it maketh rich"* (Proverbs 10:22).

But now, living in Palos Verdes wasn't to win his father's affection or approval, he was there as a testimony to God's goodness and His power to bless.

Chapter 4

I Can't Make a Speech!

Ed's teenage years were ones that found him searching for a place to fit in and somewhere to belong. He ended up joining a car club called The Continentals. (Even to this day, he can tell you the car's make and model with a healthy blurb of information about it as well.)

He had his own 1955 Ford with a '57 Chevy grill that he raced down the street, sporting stereo speakers in the grill so he could play "Blueberry Hill," and "Eddie, My Love," as he'd rock down the road, letting everyone know he was coming. He was a handsome sight with his greased curlycue hanging down his forehead and kicker platform shoes. (He had to have the right kind of shoes because they were used as a weapon when he got into a fight!)

Ed and the car club members were always out getting into fights, carrying chains, knives, and all kinds of paraphernalia. He felt tough and acted tough, but on the inside he was one scared puppy.

Others in the club followed Ed so closely that they made him the president of the car club. He was a good gang leader and never backed down to a threat.

But when the club won prizes at a car show, he was too scared to even get up in front of the people to make a speech and receive the trophy. This is a fear that Ed would encounter again when God called him to preach, but it wasn't bigger than the Greater One inside of him, and it couldn't stop him because God had empowered him.

Taught To Work

Ed's father had always been a hard worker, employed as a sheet metal man, and he instilled solid work ethics in all five of his children.

"Always be the first one on the job and the last one to leave and you'll always have a job," he would drill into them. "Don't ever just stand around on the job. When you don't have anything else to do, pick up a broom. Don't wait to be told something to do. Find something to do!"

A Lesson in Forgiveness

As a young man Ed took a job on a chicken ranch that was owned by a man named Mr. Goodwin, making 75 cents an hour for taking care of the chickens and cleaning underneath the pens. The man saw how this young boy was groping for guidance and a positive influence, so he took Ed under his wing and treated him like a son. He trained him well in the business and placed his trust in him as a faithful worker.

He knew Ed was trying to earn enough money to buy a Cushman motorcycle, so he would occasionally slip him some extra money.

One day as Ed was working in the barn, a guy who regularly delivered supplies came into the barn and began working alongside Ed. Day after day, little by little, he began making comments to Ed against Mr. Goodwin. This continued for several weeks.

"Mr. Goodwin is cheap!" the other fellow would complain. On and on the guy continued to bad-mouth Ed's boss.

Before long, Ed, who was feeding the chicks in the incubator, joined in with the fellow.

"Yeah," Ed agreed boldly, "Mr. Goodwin is cheap!" and the two began to bemoan their situation on the job. Unknown to them, Mr. Goodwin was in the tool room that was next to the incubators and heard every word they said through the wide cracks in the wall.

The next time the guy came by to make a delivery, Mr. Goodwin told him, "I'm not doing any more business with you, so get out of here!"

Now Ed stood face to face with the man who had put so much into him, the man who had taken him in and treated him like a son.

"Ed, come with me." He led Ed into his office and handed him his final paycheck.

Ed was heartbroken. He knew that he was wrong, but he had listened to the wrong people. He stood there embarrassed and ashamed that he had spoken ill of his boss who had been so good to him.

Ed gathered his stuff and got on his new Cushman motorcycle and rode home.

A few weeks later Mr. Goodwin's son drove to Ed's house. "You know, Dad really misses you and loves you. I know he would hire you back if you would just go and talk to him."

"You really think so?" Ed brightened up.

"Yeah, I know he would."

Ed hopped on his motorcycle and rode to Mr. Goodwin's as fast as he could.

He found Mr. Goodwin and started apologizing. "Uh, Mr. Goodwin, I'm sorry I said those things about you. I really didn't mean them."

"I know you didn't mean them, so I'm hiring you back. Not only that, I'm promoting you to superintendent of one of my stores and giving you a raise!"

Mr. Goodwin taught him a lesson his own heavenly Father would teach him. God is even more quick to forgive and to bless.

Chapter 5

You'll Preach the Gospel!

It was at the age of twenty-one that Ed married, and over the next six years, three daughters — Carole, Suzie, and Stephanie — were born into the family. Neither Ed nor his wife were born again at the time of their marriage, but it wasn't long until their lives and family were changed forever.

You're a Nut!

It was in 1965 that Ed Dufresne's life was to be dramatically and eternally changed. He was doing construction work at the time and was constantly being approached by a fellow worker named Billy, inviting him to church. Day after day Billy witnessed to Ed telling him how he needed to invite Jesus into his heart.

"Jesus loves you, Ed, and I love you too," Billy would tell him.

"I knew you were a nut! Men don't tell men that they love one another!" Ed's father had never told him that he loved him, so it was very hard for him to believe that someone could love him.

"Besides," Ed continued, "I'm Catholic!"

"Jesus loves Catholics," Billy answered back.

Ed didn't understand that, but he knew his life had to change.

The Gaff, a local bar, was where Ed could be found after work and on the weekends. Salary that was needed to pay bills and to buy food and clothing for his family was being spent there.

Following the path of his family members, he knew he was soon headed for the mental institution.

I Don't Need a Rag Sale, I Need Help!

In desperation for meaning and peace, Ed found himself at the Catholic church, talking with the priest. "I've got to do something with my life!" he pleaded with the priest.

"You need to get involved with the men's rag sale they have every week."

"Uh, I don't think so," Ed was stunned at the priest's suggestion.

"Well then, why don't you get involved in the men's bake sale? Or maybe you just need to go through catechism again," was the priest's counsel.

Rag sale! Bake sale! Ed thought in desperation. *I've got to do something with my life!*

Before he left the parish, the priest pushed some pamphlets on catechism into his hand, which Ed shoved in his pocket, then he promptly headed for the bar.

Little did Ed know that he was about to have an experience that would forever mark and change his life. His search for God was about to come to an end.

Desperate for help, Ed sat on the bar stool trying to wash his troubles away with one drink after another. He had done all he knew to do. He had tried everything this world has to offer — but he was still empty inside. He was hurting, desperate, and searching. He didn't know where to turn next, and the future seemed to hold only more of what he had already lived. But as he sat on that bar stool, this one particular Friday night, as Ed's heart cried out, searching for God, it was answered – *there came a sound from heaven!*

In Acts 2:1,2 it is recorded, *"And when the day of Pentecost was fully come, they were all with one accord in one place. And suddenly there came a sound from heaven...."*

This world is full of sounds, our lives are full of sounds, but in the heart of every man is a longing to hear a sound from heaven. It's the sounds that come from heaven that change a man. It's the sounds that come from heaven that change a heart. It's the sounds that come from heaven that change a home. It's the sounds that come from heaven that change a world.

Enough of the sounds that come from man's plans! No more of the sounds that come from man's ambitions! It's the sounds of heaven resounding through the soul of a God-filled man that this world needs.

It was a sound from heaven, a voice from heaven, that rang audibly in the ears of Ed Dufresne as he sat on the bar stool.

I'm Going To Be a Priest

"You'll go all over the world and preach the gospel!" boomed God's voice. Ed had never heard anything like that before! Who said that? Was it God?

Ed staggered in his mind over these words that he had

just heard. "I'll go all over the world and preach the gospel? What does that mean? Since I'm Catholic, that must mean I'm going to be a priest!" Ed reasoned.

"Hey, Joe," Ed, who was drunk by now, bellowed to the bartender, "set everybody up with a beer! I'm going to be a priest!"

As the guys were drinking the beer Ed bought for them, he walked all through the bar declaring," I'm going to be a priest! I'm going to be a priest!" Pulling the catechism pamphlets out of his pocket, he passed them around to his beer-drinking buddies. They all laughed at him, but they all drank his beer.

These People Are Rude

While on the construction site, Billy had been diligently prodding Ed to go with him to his full gospel church and Ed had finally agreed, just to get him off his back. The Sunday following his encounter with God in the bar, Ed found himself sitting in a pew in the full gospel church.

The pastor had been informed prior to the service about this Catholic visitor. What a good catch a Catholic boy would make! The preacher, who sounded to Ed like an auctioneer, preached hard and fast, hoping that the heart of this Catholic attender would be moved.

During the preaching Ed heard "amens" and "hallelujahs" ring out from all over the auditorium. *How rude*, he thought. *If I had done that in my Catholic church, the nuns would have slapped my hands.*

I've Never Heard This Before!

At one point in the service, a Filipino woman in the congregation stood to her feet, with closed eyes and hands raised. She lifted her voice and began to speak boldly in another language that Ed had never heard before.

The preacher dropped his head, thinking that this would scare the Catholic visitor away, but this, more than anything else, moved Ed's heart toward God. The hair on the back of his neck stood up! He didn't understand what was happening, but he knew this was supernatural — this was God!

When the woman finished speaking, her husband, who was sitting beside her, rose to his feet and interpreted in English what his wife had said.

A New Creature in Christ

As the service came to a close, the pastor gave an altar call, not knowing if Ed would respond. Ed could hardly wait for the altar call. He moved out of the pew and fell across the altar.

He prayed the sinner's prayer, and made Jesus the Lord of his life — everything changed at that instant! All the emptiness, confusion, and heartache were gone; joy, hope, and love had taken their place. The old Ed Dufresne died that day and a new Ed Dufresne rose up from the altar.

At last, he had found what his heart had been hungry for all his life. Life would be different now — he was a new creature in Christ!

Chapter 6
The Birth of a Ministry

The pastor had invited Ed to attend the evening service that night and instructed him to bring his Bible. He was excited as he came back through the church doors that night carrying his big, white, coffee table-size Catholic Bible under his arm.

He was warmly greeted as he came in the building, but was quickly supplied with a new copy of a *King James* Bible.

The Toilet Ministry

At the close of the evening service Ed approached the pastor and said, "I want to do something for Jesus. Is there anything I can do in the church?"

"Why, yes," came the pastor's reply. "There's no one to clean the restrooms. I've been having to clean them."

"Well, that's my job! I want to do it," came Ed's hearty response.

What a key this is to living in the blessings of God. Will you do anything for God? Will you be faithful and serve Him with joy wherever there's a need? Will you count it an honor to serve Him in the least visible position?

The day Ed got saved, he began serving God in the ministry of helps cleaning the restrooms. He was so grateful to get to do *anything* for God! He had worked hard in the past just to get a paycheck, but now that he was saved, how much more he wanted to labor in serving God.

As time passed, Ed continued to faithfully take care of cleaning the church restrooms, loving and serving God wholeheartedly, and growing in the things of God.

After several months, he proved himself faithful to God and to the pastor, and was promoted to door greeter.

When people came through the church doors, Ed Dufresne was the first person to grab their hand and give them a warm greeting: "Good to see you, brother," and "God bless you, sister."

Before long, Ed began cleaning the whole church. He vacuumed, dusted, and did any other odd jobs necessary to keep the gathering place of God's people in top condition.

How he loved and honored the work he did for God. The more he served Him, the more he loved Him. The more he loved Him, the more he served Him. He was just so thankful to be free!

Because of Ed's faithfulness, he was promoted from being a door greeter to being a church deacon. Everyone knew that Ed Dufresne was a finisher and would give everything in his service to God. And because he honored God, God honored him.

A Voice from the Pulpit

One day as Ed straightened, vacuumed, and dusted the sanctuary, setting everything in order, he made his way to the platform, continuing to clean. He walked over to the pulpit and began dusting it. As he did, something happened. Out of the pulpit came a voice — *a sound from heaven.*

"You will one day stand behind the pulpit and preach My Word," came the audible voice. Ed looked around the sanctuary to see who could possibly be in there.

Surely, he thought, *the pastor has put a speaker in the pulpit and he is playing a joke on me.* Getting down on his hands and knees, searching every inch of that pulpit, he found no speaker, no other person in the building, no pastor — *only a sound from heaven.*

Chapter 7

I'll Build It!

During this time it was decided that the congregation needed a new church building. They had outgrown their present facility, so blueprints were drawn up and steps were taken to proceed with its construction.

Since Ed was a construction worker, he was excited about the new building project. However, God began dealing with him about playing a major role in its construction. One day, while at work, God spoke to Ed, "I want you to quit your construction job and become the foreman on the church construction job." Ed knew that finances would be tight for the church and that they weren't in a position to pay him.

"But God," Ed questioned, "how am I going to make a living if I quit my job and work for free on the church construction? How will I feed my family?"

"Don't you worry about it," God assured him. "I'll take care of you!"

So Ed approached the pastor, telling him how God had dealt with him, and he offered his services to the pastor for the construction of the church.

Little did Ed know that God was training him for the years ahead when he would one day be responsible for the construction of church buildings for his own ministry.

If Ed had not taken that step to obey God, quitting his job and volunteering his services for the church, it is doubtful that he would be in the ministry he is in today. A man must be proven before God will promote him. A man must be willing to say boldly, "God has spoken and I will obey," even when that obedience doesn't make sense to the natural mind.

God never calls you to do what *you* can do, He calls you to do what only *He* can do!

Faithful to God

It is seldom that God sends the man who has his pockets full of provision to do a job. Usually, it's the man whose heart is full of faith in the Provider that God can use. Money can run out, but faith in the Provider grows.

Thank God that He does bless and prosper His children, but we obey God's call because He has spoken, not because all the circumstances are favorable for our obedience. Even when circumstances aren't what we want them to be, we obey! Circumstances will change, but only after our obedience.

As God instructed, Ed quit his job and became the foreman for the church construction job.

It was only a few days later that the kitchen cupboards became bare and food became scarce.

"God," Ed reminded Him, "You told me to quit my job and work on the church building. I'm doing that, but my family doesn't have food and I don't have money. What am I to do?"

"There's good, day-old food behind the grocery store," God answered.

So when it got dark, Ed drove behind the local grocery store and found bread, tomatoes, and other discarded food that was perfectly good.

After several nights of collecting the day-old food, the store's produce man caught Ed behind the store.

"So, you're the one who's been taking all the food from back here," he stated.

"Yes, it's been me," Ed confessed, "I hope it's all right."

"Sure," came the reply. "In fact, I'll have a special supply of food back here for you every night. You just come by and pick it up."

So, for several months, Ed's family was supplied with good food at no cost to them.

A Business of His Own

As the weeks passed, there came an opportunity for Ed to work a night job doing a cleaning service for business offices. Little did Ed know that this was part of God's plan for his life.

Ed worked nights doing building maintenance, then he worked during the day on the church construction.

After a short time, his employer on the building maintenance job left the business and the customers were requesting Ed to take over their accounts. The customers were so pleased with his work that they even furnished him with all his cleaning equipment until he was able to purchase his own.

It was supernatural how God set Ed up in his own maintenance business, which grew to the point he had to employ fifteen additional workers. God used this business to teach him many principles of faith, as well as meet his financial needs.

Chapter 8

He's Got His Own Gang

While in a church service one evening, a visiting minister called Ed forward from the congregation and said, "The angels of God are protecting your life."

The night he received that word, Ed went to work on the night shift of his building maintenance business. He was driving down the road when he saw a gang of guys grab a girl and her brother. Ed quickly turned the truck around to go get them. He drove by, threw his truck door open and yelled at the girl and her brother to jump in. The brother jumped in and slammed the door, leaving his sister to the gang. "Go on, get out of here!" the guy yelled to Ed.

"No, I'm not leaving that girl with those guys!" Ed turned the truck around, slammed on his brakes, and jumped out of the truck. When he jumped out of the truck, the guy inside locked the doors and wouldn't let Ed back in.

"Let that girl go!" Ed yelled to the gang.

The gang turned in his direction and headed toward Ed while pulling out chains and other gang weapons. Ed stood there alone in front of his truck, holding no weapon, no plan of how to rescue the girl, with an angry, armed gang coming closer.

As Ed stood facing the oncoming hoodlums, the leader suddenly stopped, pointed Ed's way and began to yell. "Hey,

39

he's got his own gang! Let's get out of here!" They turned and took off running, leaving the girl behind.

Ed looked behind him. He was standing there alone, so he thought!

The word the minister had given him that night had come to pass. The angels were protecting him.

Chapter 9
Anointed with Healing Power

A day of great celebration came when the church building was finally completed. Ed and others had worked long, hard hours to bring it to completion and Ed was thrilled to be able to do his part and to serve God using his God-given abilities. Ed has always said, "If you don't know what you can do to serve God, just serve in the area of your abilities and then your supernatural abilities will kick in."

Ed was growing stronger in God simply because he was willing to serve God with all that he possessed.

A Vision of Calvary

During the building dedication service, Ed stood along the altar area, lined up with all the deacons. It was the time of the service when the congregation was to receive communion together; the deacons held the emblems of communion and the pastor began praying. While this was going on, Ed lifted his heart toward God.

"What does all this mean? I want to understand what communion means," Ed prayed from his own heart.

All of a sudden, God opened Ed's eyes and he saw a vision. The roof of the church building disappeared and he saw Calvary. He saw Jesus hanging on the cross with two other crosses, one on either side. His appearance was so marred, just as Isaiah saw, that He didn't even look like a man.

As Ed watched the vision, he saw words begin to fly through the air and strike Jesus. CANCER, TUBERCULOSIS, DIABETES, BLINDNESS. . . . The words struck Jesus and each time a word struck him, He jolted and His appearance was marred even more.

As Ed watched, the words began flying faster and faster toward Him through the air. All these diseases were laid on Him. Names of every disease known to man, and even diseases that are still unknown to man — diseases yet to be birthed by hell — were laid upon Jesus. He paid the price for them all, for Scripture says that Jesus healeth *ALL* our diseases (Psalm 103:3).

Within moments the vision disappeared, but its revelation has fueled the healing ministry that God has entrusted to Ed. He has traveled millions of miles proclaiming the truth of God's Word that was seen in that vision: *"Himself took our infirmities, and bare our sicknesses"* (Matthew 8:17). *" . . . by whose* [His] *stripes ye were healed"* (1 Peter 2:24).

Jesus Is the Healer

God began revealing the truths of His Word to Ed in a new way and he grew leaps and bounds spiritually. Then one day, Ed got hold of a message that changed his life and his life's course was forever set. Someone loaned him a used copy of T. L. Osborn's book, *Healing the Sick*. The book was so worn that it was held together with wide, black electrical tape.

The truths contained in that book ignited a fire in Ed to see God's people healed and set free from all that would endeavor to yoke them. How the message of healing burned in his heart! He had never heard anything like this preached. In fact, the doctrine he was hearing from the pulpit was that God was the One who made people sick to teach them something.

But when God brought the message of divine healing to light in Ed's life, his heart grabbed it with an unshakable grip. No amount of doubt or unbelief in what was being preached could make him doubt God's Word on the truth of healing.

Sell Your House

It was during this time in 1971 that Ed got a pamphlet advertising a Full Gospel Businessmen's Meeting that was to be held in the Hilton Hotel in Denver, Colorado. He had never heard of the ministers who were going to be there, but he knew he was to attend. The only problem was, he didn't have the money to make the trip.

As Ed was working on the roof of the new church building one day, he prayed, "Lord, I sure would like to go to that Denver Convention. I ask You to supply me with the means to go."

God gave him the answer. "Sell your house."

When Ed heard God's instruction to him, it startled him and he lost his footing. He began sliding off the roof of the church and landed on the ground below, breaking his back. Workers came running from all directions.

"Be still, we'll call an ambulance," were the orders being shouted by those standing by.

Ed knew that his back was broken, but God had been teaching him about divine healing.

"No, don't call an ambulance, I'm healed!" He began to get up.

"No, lie back down and be still. We've got to get you to the hospital," they cautioned.

"No," Ed insisted, "I'm healed."

As Ed put forth the effort to get up, the power of God hit him. The others looked on in amazement as they saw him walk away unhurt from such a bad fall.

Over the next few days, Ed did as God instructed him and put his house on the market. The Full Gospel Businessmen's Meeting in Denver, Colorado, would be held in a little over a month, so it would take God's intervention to sell and close on the house in time for Ed to have the money to go to the meetings. But God had spoken and His word to Ed came to pass. The house was sold as soon as he put it on the market and he had the money in hand within thirty days.

Ed was on his way to Denver, Colorado!

How important it is that we obey God! We don't always know the reasons God may tell us to do some things, but we can be assured of this — it is so we can be blessed. We don't know the future as He does, so we must follow Him closely today so that we will be prepared for the future.

It looked like Ed was suffering decrease because he no longer owned a home, but God was leading him into increase

— spiritual increase, which brought increase in every other area of his life as well.

Kenneth E. Hagin, Sr. states, "Payday isn't every day, but payday will come!"

It pays to obey God! It pays to obey, even when you don't fully understand. Increase is on the way. Pay the price to be ready for it.

The Preacher in Cowboy Boots

When he arrived at the hotel he found out the names of those who were scheduled to minister — men he had never heard of before. There was a man named John Osteen, another named Kenneth E. Hagin, Sr. and a man from Texas who wore cowboys boots, Kenneth Copeland.

There were several meetings going on at one time. While one minister was conducting services in the main auditorium, another one would be holding a service in another meeting room.

Ed had heard that Kenneth Copeland was going to be conducting a youth meeting in the basement, the room called The Dungeon, and he knew he had to be in that meeting.

As Ed was wondering how to get admitted into the youth meeting, a man he knew, who was supposed to sing in the meeting, walked by. "Hey," Ed stopped him, "do you think you can get me into that youth meeting?"

"Sure," the singer agreed. "Come with me."

Ed followed him into the auditorium and sat down on the front row with him.

The service started and Kenneth Copeland got up to preach. Ed had never heard anyone preach like this man! He made the Bible come alive! He stomped all across the front of that auditorium, preaching his heart out to the youth who packed out that room. He walked back and forth across the platform, preaching about the young covenant man, David.

What Ed heard that day changed his life! He had never heard a message like that! He didn't know he had a covenant that would slay any giant that tried to taunt him in life.

I've got to hear more of this, Ed thought to himself. *I've never heard anyone preach with such authority!* The message that day lodged deep into Ed's heart. Life for him was only going higher. This anointed message from this God-filled man had brought him into a new place in God and in His Word.

As soon as the meeting was over, Ed rushed out to the lobby to buy any tapes this man had for sale. Ed asked around, "Does that fella named Kenneth Copeland have any preaching tapes available?"

Behind him he heard a woman's reply, "Yes, he does. Here's a catalog of his tapes."

Ed turned around to take the catalog from the small blonde-haired woman, who he found out was Gloria Copeland.

She went on to explain that her husband had been booked to minister in these meetings at the last minute, so he was unable to bring any of his tapes with him.

Ed tucked the tape catalog safely away, and when he returned home to California, he ordered every tape Brother Copeland offered. Ed locked himself up in the garage and spent hour after hour listening to those reel-to-reel tapes. The message of God's Word on those tapes propelled him toward God's will for his life and ministry.

Ed had no way of knowing that in decades to come, he would share in such a rich fellowship with him.

Ed has cherished the opportunity to sit under his ministry.

Healing Power in His Hand

As the Full Gospel Businessmen's meetings continued, Ed's life was radically changed by the Word he heard from these men of God. It was also during these meetings that Ed first heard Kenneth E. Hagin, Sr., who was to become his spiritual father. These were landmark meetings in Ed's life in so many ways.

As Ed was walking through the Hilton lobby to attend another meeting, he saw a friend of his, a gospel singer, standing on some steps that led to an auditorium with his hands raised, praising the Lord. But there was a lady lying on the floor in front of the singer and people were beginning to gather around. Ed was concerned that something might be wrong with the woman.

"Hey," Ed asked the singer, "what's wrong with the lady?"

"Oh, nothing," he answered. "She just asked me to lay hands on her to receive the baptism of the Holy Spirit, and she fell out in the Spirit." Up to this time Ed had never seen anyone slain in the Spirit. That was all new to him, but he didn't doubt that it was the power of God.

"Oh, God," Ed whispered silently, "I hope You never do anything like that to me in front of all these. . . ."

BAM! Ed hit the floor as a bright light flashed around him.

The power of God fell on him and he landed sprawled out across the steps, alongside the woman on the steps, but it didn't stop there! An obese woman wearing a tent dress fell right on top of him! (Ed testifies that this was the day he got delivered from any prejudice against woman preachers.) And about fifty people who were standing around them fell like dominoes all over the lobby floor.

As he lay there alongside one woman, with another one sprawled out on top of him and a crowd lying around, a phenomenon happened -- his right hand started burning, then Jesus spoke to him, "I am placing a healing anointing in your hand. You are called to the healing ministry."

Finally, the woman alongside him got up, then the obese lady on top of him got up.

"Jesus did something to you!" the obese woman exclaimed. "Yes, He did. My whole arm is burning and He told me that it was a healing anointing in my hand." Ed described the experience to her.

"Lay your hands on me," the woman urged him. I've got a huge cancerous tumor around my mid-section. That's why I'm so big and I have to wear this tent-shaped dress. Lay your hands on me!"

With God's healing power in his hand, Ed laid his right hand on the woman.

When he touched her it looked like someone stuck a pin

in that huge tumor. The tumor around her mid-section instantly disappeared right before everyone's eyes and that tent dress fell straight alongside her body.

Ed stood back in shock! He had never seen anything like that before! The woman began shouting and praising the Lord, along with the others who had gathered together.

"Young whippersnapper," an elderly man called, making his way up from the outer edge of the crowd, "lay your hand on me to receive the Holy Ghost!"

Ed put his hand on him and the elderly man immediately began speaking in tongues.

"I've been seeking for the Holy Ghost for fifty years!" he exclaimed.

One after another, people from all over the hotel lobby asked Ed to lay his hands on them. People were being slain in the Holy Spirit and laying all over the floor of that lobby.

Healings were taking place everywhere! He laid hands on people for an hour and a half.

"Get him his own meeting room!" someone yelled from the crowd.

Was it worth it to sell his home to attend a meeting?

Divine Appointments

How many have missed divine appointments of impartation because they wouldn't pay the price to be where God told them to be? How many have found it easier to stay at home rather than be inconvenienced to travel to be where God's power is in manifestation? How many times has someone been content to read a book or listen to a tape rather than to be around a man of God in a meeting?

In the final years of his life, Dr. Lester Sumrall preached all over the world, proclaiming that the greatest revival this world has ever seen will be in China.

Smith Wigglesworth, an English minister, laid his hands on the young Lester Sumrall and prophesied, "I won't live to see it, but you will. You will see the last great move of God."

Dr. Sumrall testified everywhere, "I'm seeing it, the greatest move of God on earth! It's in China! People are getting saved and healed by the thousands. They are raising people from the dead on a regular basis. Hundreds have been raised from the dead. I continue to travel to China again and again just so I can be in the move of God."

Even in his eighties, after more than sixty years of ministry, Lester Sumrall never quit paying the price to be where God was moving in the earth. He professed that he prayed the same prayer every day of his life, "Lord, don't do anything great in the earth today without letting me be right in the middle of it!"

He certainly meant it when he prayed that prayer, because he would travel anywhere in the earth on a moment's notice to experience heaven's outpouring.

After more than sixty years of ministry, the move of God, the outpouring of God, the impartations of God, never became common to him. He continued to seek to know God more until his last day on this earth.

He so honored God and the moves of God, that as a man

in his eighties, he would still pay any price to go to an inconvenient place to receive more from God.

You can't receive all God has for you while sitting in your own home. Will you pay any price to be where God is moving?

You don't have to wait for God to tell you to go there. Go there because you're hungry! Go there because you want more! Go there because you want to be a better minister! Go there because you want to be a greater blessing! Be where God is manifesting Himself!

"What is man, that thou art mindful of him? and the son of man, that thou VISITEST him?" (Psalm 8:4).

We know God is mindful of us because He visits us. How does God visit mankind? Martin Luther was a visitation from God. John Wesley was a visitation from God. Smith Wigglesworth was a visitation from God. John G. Lake was a visitation from God. Dr. Lester Sumrall was a visitation from God. All of God's holy ministers are a visitation from God.

Heaven visits men through God-soaked vessels. Your pastor is a visitation from God in your life. Be faithful to a local church; be a blessing and serve in your local church. It doesn't matter if you stand in a fivefold office or if you are a layman in the body of Christ, you're not in the will of God unless you're faithful to a local church, submitted to a pastor and serving in that local body in some capacity.

Even those in full-time ministry should have a local church they are faithful to, both in attendance and in service.

The Word tells us that the sheep fainted and were scattered abroad, because they had no shepherd (Matthew 9:36). A pastor is an adhesive force in the life of the sheep; he keeps them from being scattered. He keeps their finances, children, marriages, health, and homes from being scattered.

We must honor what God honors. We must place our honor on the things God honors.

The Bible, in speaking about the twin brothers Esau and Jacob, says that God loved Jacob but He hated Esau; He lightly esteemed Esau (Malachi 1:2,3).

Why was that?

Jacob carried an honor for the things of God, but Esau treated lightly the things God held as honorable.

Esau exchanged his birthright for something natural, a bowl of soup. Jacob honored that birthright and fixed his heart on acquiring it.

Someone else will acquire what was meant for you if you don't esteem it as valuable and treat it with honor.

Yet, if we're not careful, we can exchange our divine appointments with God for a last minute, natural crisis that keeps us away from the place where God is moving.

Dr. Sumrall carried a rich anointing on his life because he always honored and pursued the move of God. He would pay any price to receive more of the most valuable thing one can possess – the anointing of God.

No one knows what Thomas was doing or where he was the day all the other disciples were gathered and Jesus appeared to them and breathed upon them (John 20:19-31). Because Thomas missed being at the gathering place of the other disciples and refused to believe that Jesus had appeared to them, this world knows him as "doubting Thomas." He just failed to be at the right place at the right time. How many times have we allowed the unimportant to take preeminence over the spiritual?

Jesus appeared to many after His resurrection, and at one time He even appeared to as many as 500 people (1 Corinthians 15:6). His message to them was to go to Jerusalem and wait there until they received the Holy Spirit (Luke 24:49, Acts 1:4,5). We know that He instructed more than just His twelve disciples to gather in Jerusalem to receive the Holy Spirit because there were 120 gathered together in the upper room on the Day of Pentecost. They were there because of His instructions to them.

But where were the other 380 people? Some were working in their fields. Some were at their jobs. Some were running errands. But only 120 were where the wind was blowing and the fire was falling (Acts 2).

Will you be where God wants you to be, whatever inconveniences you have to walk over to get there?

Ed Dufresne paid what some would call an extreme price to be where God was moving. What was his reward? The priceless healing anointing.

Ed returned home a different man.

Chapter 10

Come Out from Among Them

Word spread quickly through Ed's home church about the healings that were taking place when he laid his hands on the sick. All kinds of notable healings were happening. Even severe scars were instantly disappearing from people's bodies.

Ed taught a Sunday school class in his church since he was a deacon. After he returned home from the Convention, he fed daily on Word tapes, so he gave that Sunday school class a diet of the Word they had never tasted before.

He knew people would be thrilled and blessed to hear that God was still in the healing business. He knew people would be joyous to learn about living by faith. However, this wasn't the case. One after another, church members confronted him concerning the message of faith and divine healing.

Every time he went to church, the once popular, well-loved deacon was avoided like the plague. The brethren would walk down the opposite aisle in the sanctuary just to avoid him and to keep from having to shake his hand.

During one Sunday morning service, as he passed the offering bucket down the aisle, a woman sitting on the end of the pew blurted out, "I'll have you to know that my mother was a woman of God. She prayed and read her Bible every day of her life, and it *was* the will of God for her to be sick and die!"

Ed stood in the aisle with everyone glaring at him. "Well, ma'am, I'm not the one who said it is the will of God for the sick to be healed and to live — God's the One who said it. You don't have a problem with me. You have a problem with God! He's the One who wants everyone healed!"

It wasn't long before his Sunday school class was taken away from him and he was given the children's class to teach.

Actually, with the kids is where Ed could accomplish something! He began teaching them about faith and how to lay hands on the sick. His children's class quickly grew from thirty kids to one hundred and fifty kids. He taught them to pray for the kids in their schools, and that's just what they did!

One of Ed's students told a crippled classmate at his Christian school that God wanted to heal him. The classmate, who was born without a hip socket and joint, had never walked normally and had to use a crutch. He excitedly agreed to be prayed for.

As Ed's student put his hands on the boy's hip and prayed, a sound like that of a shotgun could be heard. BAM! God put a new hip in the boy's body.

News of the boy's healing spread like wildfire through the church. Everyone was in an uproar! Not with rejoicing, but with anger.

"Who do you think you are teaching that stuff to our kids? Do you think we believe in that stuff?" they blazed out at Ed.

It was apparent that everyone didn't embrace this message that had changed Ed Dufresne's life.

Ed was baffled! Why do people fight to stay sick? Why do they refuse to believe that God is good?

Greater and greater opposition came to him from the church members. They became colder and colder to him, shunning him at every service. Then they took the children's class away from him, letting him know that they wanted no part of the faith and healing message he was preaching.

One particular man in the church had violently opposed Ed and mocked the message of healing that he was sharing. But one evening he showed up on Ed's front porch with two large dogs and he was crying hysterically. "Brother Ed, do you think God would heal my dogs? They were both in the street and got hit; their backs are crushed." The man was heartbroken over the dogs he loved so much.

"Yes," Ed replied. "God will heal your dogs just because He loves you."

Ed placed his hands on the backs of both of the dogs. The healing anointing shot into their bodies and bones could be heard as they popped and were put back into place. The dogs leaped up perfectly whole.

The man and Ed rejoiced together as they saw how God's power will bless everything that touches our lives.

Still, those in the church opposed and shunned Ed and he knew it was time to leave; there was nothing else that he could do.

It broke his heart to leave the church that had brought him

to Christ. He had dearly loved, honored, and served his pastor, but it was time to go.

Chapter 11

I'll Never Preach Again!

It wasn't long until God opened doors for Ed Dufresne to minister publicly. But Ed had such great difficulty with getting up in front of people. As the president of The Continentals' Car Club, he couldn't even get up in front of people to receive the trophies they won. How was he ever going to be able to get up in front of a congregation to preach?

He had seldom received any encouragement toward having a pulpit ministry. The only thing he had ever been told was, "You'll have to go to speech class for ten years just so you'll quit messing up your words; then you'll have to go to Bible school."

Ten years of speech class, then Bible school! How could he ever become a preacher?

Toting a Tape Player

As he was invited to minister to some smaller groups of people, he devised a plan so that he wouldn't have to be concerned about preaching.

He knew that Jesus had placed a tangible healing anointing in his right hand, so he felt comfortable in laying hands on the sick to transmit that healing power into their bodies — just so long as he didn't have to preach!

As he walked into the room where he was invited to conduct his first service, he didn't come alone. He had the Holy Spirit, his Bible, a tape player, and Kenneth Copeland — on tape!

When Ed was introduced to those assembled, he walked to the pulpit with his tape player in hand, placed the tape player on the pulpit and inserted Brother Copeland's tape.

"Brother Copeland is going to preach to you, then when the message is over, I'll come back to the front and lay hands on those of you who need healing." He turned the tape player on, then took his seat and listened with the congregation to Brother Copeland's message.

When the tape came to an end, Ed walked back up to the front, turned off the tape player, then invited those who needed healing to come forward.

After they lined up, he went to each of them and laid hands on them. One person after another was slain in the Spirit and then rose up to find their bodies healed. Some testified to feeling heat in the afflicted areas of their bodies. Others felt what they described as bolts of lightning surge through them. They all rejoiced in what God had done for them, but they had never seen anyone conduct a service like Ed Dufresne!

Every time Ed went to minister, he totted his tape player and Brother Copeland with him. God would bless the people and many were being healed. Brother Copeland and Ed made an unbeatable team, but it was a union that wasn't to continue long — at least in that format.

Leave Your Tape Player at Home

One day, as Ed was preparing to conduct a service, God spoke to him, "Leave your tape player at home! I want *you* to do the preaching!"

"Oh, God." Ed argued, "You know I'm not a public speaker. I stutter and stumble all over my words when I get up in front of people. I'll just minister healing to the sick."

"Leave your tape player at home!" God instructed. So with dread, Ed proceeded to the meeting.

What was he to do? What was he to say? "I can't preach to these people. I'm not a public speaker!" he repeatedly argued with God.

At last it was time for the service to begin. He stood before the people, trembling and shaking all over. He opened his mouth to speak, but he messed up his words and the further he went, the more frustrated he became. After a short time of stumbling through his sermon, he called those forward who needed healing and laid hands on them. After ministering to them, he dismissed the people and then, in humiliation, slipped off to a back room in the building and shut the door.

I'm Not a Public Speaker

"That's it!" Ed exclaimed to God. "I told you I'm not a public speaker! I messed up my words so bad and stumbled all over the place! I'm never going to preach again! That's it!"

As he had it out with God, there came a soft knock on the door and a woman slowly stuck her head into the room where Ed was.

"Brother Dufresne, can I talk to you a minute?"

"I guess so," Ed replied half humiliated and half embarrassed.

"I wanted to show you my little girl's foot. She had a club foot, but while you were preaching, it began to straighten out and now it's perfectly normal."

Ed sat there dumbfounded. He couldn't believe that God had done *that* while he was preaching *that* sermon. In spite of his flaws, God had moved and this little girl was miraculously healed.

The woman and the little girl left the room and Ed sat there not knowing what to say next to God.

A few minutes later there came another knock on the door. "Brother Dufresne, I wanted to tell you that while you were preaching tonight, God healed my little boy's leg. He had a deformed kneecap and a crippled leg, but now he's healed!"

God did all that, Ed thought in amazement. *Even while I was messing up all my words. Forgive me, God, for being so focused on myself!*

God showed Ed that it isn't man's ability or inability that blesses and touches people, but it is God and His mighty power that changes lives. It's not what man can do that's important, but it's what God can do that counts.

It was a lesson he never forgot.

On the Road

From that time forward, Ed began receiving other invitations to minister.

He would drive hours and hours to preach to a handful of people, but God was teaching him the joy of trusting Him. There were many times when he left his home with barely enough food to feed the family and only enough gas money in his pocket to reach the place where he was to preach.

He would preach his heart out and receive only enough money to make it to his next preaching engagement.

As he drove from one church to the next to preach, he would be playing reel-to-reel tapes on his old Realistic tape player that was loaded with 'D' cell batteries. He listened by the hour to Kenneth E. Hagin, Sr. and Kenneth Copeland. He was so hungry to hear the Word of God and ready to act on it, letting others know what God has done in his life.

Running out of gas, sporting empty pockets and driving an old Buick with four bald tires, he drove from city to city, letting people know that Jesus the Healer is still healing today.

"Stupid, stupid, stupid, stupid!" the four bald tires seemed to sing as they spun down the highway. The devil would bombard his mind, "You're crazy for leaving your family at home with little food and little money." But the devil was too late to change this man's mind! The Word had changed his life and no opposition could make him turn back now. Full speed ahead!

Look Into the Future

In one city in California where he was to preach, he was taken to a vacant home by the church leadership and told he could lodge there during his stay. The owner had recently died in the house and the family had cleaned it out, leaving it vacant. They did leave a bed in one of the downstair's rooms for him, but he felt terribly alone in the vacant home.

That night he went to the church and preached, then returned to the vacant home. As he settled down to go to bed, a bright light suddenly filled the room! He looked up to see an angel standing in the room, and the angel pointed to a window on the opposite wall, saying, "Look into the future. See what's to come in your ministry."

With those words, the bed he was in moved to the opposite wall and landed right up against the open window. Looking through this window he didn't see what was outside. Instead, he saw what was in the future.

He found himself looking down on a large platform in an auditorium filled with thousands of people. He was the minister on the platform and he was conducting a massive healing crusade.

At that point, the vision ended, the window into the future closed, the angel disappeared, and the room returned to normal.

Chapter 12

The Young Pastor

Those early years were ones that fortified faithfulness into Ed Dufresne's life. No matter how hard the circumstances were, he learned never to quit. No matter how hard the road seemed, he kept going. No matter how strong the opposition, he kept pressing. No matter how difficult the circumstances, he never gave up!

Ed's road of faithfulness would lead him to many ministry opportunities, one of which included preaching to the Indians in Oregon for a year. This and other experiences all played a vital part in the shaping of God's man.

Not only was Ed strong in preaching the message of faith and divine healing, but his services were also marked by the move of the Holy Spirit, especially his miracle services known as "Jesus the Healer Rallies." All kinds of miracles and healings took place, and people who needed healing came from everywhere to have hands laid on them.

Ministering to the Deaf

It was through one of Ed's "Jesus the Healer Rallies" that more impartations came. While Ed was ministering to those who were in the healing line, he walked up in front of two people who held up signs for him to read. "We are deaf mutes.

Can you help us?" Compassion welled up in Ed as he ministered to them.

As he was later thinking about those two people, God spoke to him, "I'm giving you a special anointing to minister healing to the deaf." From that time forward many deaf cases have been healed through Ed's ministry.

Yielding to the compassion of God will result in greater manifestations of the healing power of God.

His First Church

As time passed, word came from God in the 1970's to start a church in Torrance, California.

By this time, God had taught Ed Dufresne many things about living a life of faith. The Word of Faith message was being thrust to the forefront and God had brought some of the leading faith teachers in the body of Christ across Ed's path.

In 1971 Ed became acquainted with Kenneth E. Hagin, Sr.'s ministry and what Ed has received through his life, ministry, and anointing has been immeasurable. With all love, respect, and honor, Kenneth E. Hagin, Sr. is held as the spiritual father of Ed Dufresne, and he will always be honored in the Dufresne home.

With Brother Hagin, and other leading teachers of the message of faith speaking into Ed's life, Ed's message of faith and his stand on God's Word were without compromise.

This bold ministry of faith was just what was needed in Southern California. When the church began, you could count on one hand the number of Word of Faith churches in the United

States, but Ed's church was one of those first churches. The flow of people into this new church continually increased and before too long, their storefront building was filled to capacity. People were coming from everywhere to be taught the Word of God with signs, wonders, and miracles following.

It's imperative that believers be taught what belongs to them as a part of the family of God. Although all of God's blessings are ours, without proper teaching, we won't understand what is ours; and without understanding we won't walk in the fullness of God's blessings.

The teaching of God's Word brings us the knowledge and the faith to be able to understand what God has provided for us and how we must exercise faith to receive what is ours.

Jesus Walks In

The church was growing rapidly and the traveling portion of Ed's ministry was also beginning to flourish. It was during this time that God began dealing with Ed about starting a Bible school. Ed did start the school and it was filled to capacity, ending up with well over 500 students. It was into this setting that another sound from heaven came.

The guest minister, who was speaking at the Bible school graduation, had just finished his message, and Ed walked toward the pulpit. As he reached the pulpit the power of God came on him and he fell out in the Spirit.

This is an event that was similar to an experience recorded about the life of Saul in Acts 9:3,4. *"And as he [Saul] journeyed, he came near Damascus: and suddenly there shined round about him a light from heaven: and HE FELL TO THE EARTH, and heard a voice saying unto him. . . ."*

As Ed raised himself off the floor, he looked off to the side to see Jesus walking into the auditorium through the swinging doors to the right of the platform.

Standing by the swinging doors was a fellow minister. When Jesus passed him, Ed saw Jesus put His hand on the minister, lift him up and hang him in midair against the wall with his feet unable to touch the floor, just as if he were hanging on a coat rack. Jesus then walked toward the platform and stood in front of Ed. "Be faithful in the healing ministry," Jesus began, then continued to speak with him about the ministry he was called to. Then Jesus turned to walk out.

Before Jesus reached the swinging doors, he reached out His hand, touched the minister who was still hanging against the wall and the minister fell to the floor. Jesus then exited through the swinging doors — without them opening!

Chapter 13
That's Our Building

When it came time for the congregation to move to a larger facility, they secured a building that was in an industrial park area. They needed a building use permit from the city, but knowing that God had led them to their new location, they were confident that there wouldn't be a problem in securing it.

When it was time for the city to rule on giving them their permit, Ed urged the congregation to attend the city council meeting in support of a favorable ruling.

On the night of the meeting, the congregation crowded into the meeting room of the city council in support of their pastor.

As discussion began on whether or not they would pass on giving a church a building use permit in an industrial park area, the council was aware of the importance of their decision, for it would set the precedence since a permit of its kind had never been issued in the city of Torrance.

We Have To Vote Again, the Machine Jammed

The council started discussing the pros and cons of issuing such a permit. Finally, the mayor rose to his feet. "I don't think it's a very good idea for a church to be in that location. The airport is only a short distance from there and my concern is that if an airplane were unable to reach the runway, it would crash into that church building and kill all the people in it."

The congregation sat in disbelief at the mayor's statement. Ed rose to his feet in reply, "Well, Mayor, it seems a little peculiar that you would have a concern like that since just this week you were part of the dedication ceremony of the new city hospital that is located right at the end of the runway, which is much closer to the airport than our facility."

"Well," the mayor burst out, "I'm voting against it anyway!" With that, the voting of the city council began.

One by one the council members cast their vote. The congregation was sure that the council would vote in their favor, for their pastor had stood before them time and time again reassuring them that God had told him that that was their building. As the votes were being cast, the church members were praying in tongues under their breath.

When the votes were all counted, they had lost! The church lost getting their building use permit by one vote! The congregation suddenly got quiet, quit praying in tongues, and turned their eyes toward their pastor.

Ed stood in the middle of the room, dumbfounded by the outcome. How could this happen? He was sure that God had told him that this building was theirs.

"Wait a minute!" the court reporter spoke up. "My machine jammed and I was unable to record everyone's vote. We have to vote again!"

At that moment a councilman blurted out, "Oh, I'm changing my vote. Give them the permit!" It was the one vote they needed. The congregation began rejoicing and God had once again proven faithful to His Word.

We Need a Miracle

God faithfully blessed the church and the congregation continued to grow. The building they leased, with the option to buy, escalated in value and was worth triple of what they had leased it for. The congregation needed to raise $126,000 to secure the option. Several months before the money was due, they only had $10,000 in the building account. They needed a miracle to raise the balance. If they were unable to pick up the option on the building, it would go back to the landlord, which is what he wanted since the building had now tripled in value. If they wanted to pay the whole building off, it would cost them $500,000.

As Ed prayed about the situation, God said, "Sow the $10,000 you have into the building funds of other churches."

"Give away the only $10,000 we have?" Ed questioned. "Well," he reasoned, "$10,000 won't help much anyway when you need $126,000. I might as well sow it!"

So he took the $10,000 and sowed it into other churches. With a zero balance in the church building account, Ed told God, "We're trusting You to meet our need."

One day some businessmen in the church approached Ed. "There are 126 businessmen in the congregation who will give $1,000 to the building fund which will give you the $126,000 needed to pick up the option on the building, and then the 126 businessmen can hold the papers on the building."

Ed went to the Lord. "What about this? It's the only option I appear to have. Should I agree to the offer these businessmen are making me?"

"You're having problems with *one* landlord! What do you think you're going to do with *126* of them?" God set the record straight.

Ed knew that was no solution, so he declined their offer.

We've Come To Straighten Out Your Finances

Two months before the money was due, Ed traveled to minister in a meeting in another state. He was getting dressed for the morning service when God spoke to him, "Have another minister do the meeting this morning and you stay in your room. I'm going to talk to you."

Ed called the other minister and arranged for him to conduct the morning service. Ed stayed in his room and walked back and forth as he prayed.

He was still partially dressed for the morning service he was supposed to conduct, when he heard the door to his hotel room open.

Being a veteran traveler by now, he was well-acquainted with the fact that people at the front desk would sometimes accidentally double-book the rooms and people would often come walking right into his room.

Startled to hear his door open, he swung around to see who came in. When he turned, he saw two huge angels standing in the room. The ceiling of the room seemed to disappear and the heads of the angels were well above where the ceiling would have been.

One of the angels was holding a huge sword. The other had on a breastplate that had dents and marks in it, showing that the angel had been engaged in warfare.

The angels declared, "We have been sent from the throne room of heaven to straighten out your finances!" Then the angels stood still.

Ed questioned, "What are you waiting for?"

"We are waiting for the faith command!" came their response.

Then Ed was reminded of the passage in Psalm 103:20, *"Bless the Lord, ye his angels, that excel in strength, that do his commandments, HEARKENING UNTO THE VOICE OF HIS WORD."*

Ed knew that the angels hear and obey the Word that is spoken in faith, so he boldly declared, "My God meets all my needs according to His riches in glory by Christ Jesus, so go! Bring in the money!" (Philippians 4:19)

When he spoke those words, the angels disappeared.

God's Never Late

Three days before the money was due, there was still no money in the building fund. Ed was meeting in his office with his lawyer, going over their building lease to see if there was any possible way to get an extension on the payment due date.

"No, no," the lawyer shook his head, "there's nothing more

that we can do. If you don't give the landlord $126,000 in three days, you will lose the building."

"Pastor Dufresne," the secretary paged Ed on intercom, "there is a man here to see you regarding the money due on the building."

"You go out and talk to him," Ed urged the lawyer. "I don't know who it could be and I don't want to get cornered by someone with a lot of questions about the building."

The lawyer walked out to speak with the visitor, but returned to Ed's office in a few moments. "I think you need to meet with this man. I believe he can help you," the lawyer insisted.

"Okay," Ed agreed reluctantly.

Ed walked out and met a man, dressed in a jogging suit. "I attend a different church in town. I've been to your church before, but I don't like your preaching — you scare me. You move around too much and you don't stay behind the pulpit. But God told me to come here and give you this cashier's check for $126,000."

As the man handed Ed the check, Ed rejoiced and knew that those two angels had completed their assignment and God had once again proven Himself faithful to His Word and answered the faith of a man who stood on His Word.

Sir, Obey God

A couple of weeks later, Ed had a guest minister at his church on a Sunday night. During the service, the guest minister stood on the edge of the platform and pointed toward the back of the auditorium at a man. "You sir, in the back. Come up here and obey God. Do what God told you to do."

Ed looked around to see who the minister was talking to. To Ed's astonishment, he was pointing right at the man who gave the church the $126,000. Ed tried to get the minister's attention, "He already obeyed God!"

The man came up the aisle toward the front of the church and took the microphone. "God has been dealing with me the past few days to just pay off the whole building. Give me a couple of days and I'll give you a check for $374,000!"

True to his word, within a few days, he gave Ed another check, this time for $374,000. That amount combined with the $126,000 made $500,000, which was the purchase price for the building.

"God," Ed inquired, "why did You have this man pay off the whole building? I didn't even ask You for it. I was just believing You for the $126,000 we needed immediately."

"Just because you wouldn't compromise!" God replied.

It never pays to go the route of reason, for then you'll never reach your destination. The route of faith will always take you farther and it will fulfill the will of God.

God blessed the church and it continued to grow. God's sheep also continued to grow stronger in the Word and in their faith.

Chapter 14

Impartations

In the 1970's, Ed went to a meeting in Hawaii that Brother Hagin was conducting. As Brother Hagin was ministering, the Spirit of the Lord came on him and he fell out in the Spirit behind the pulpit. Some of those in attendance rushed forward to come to his aid, thinking that something was physically wrong with him. However, those who knew Brother Hagin's ministry assured them that he was perfectly fine, but that he was under the power of the Holy Spirit.

When the Spirit of God moves strongly upon someone, their flesh will sometimes give way under God's mighty power and they will fall to the ground. All through the Bible we see recorded time and again many accounts of this occurring.

As Brother Hagin laid on the floor under the power of the Holy Spirit, God instructed him to lay hands on all the ministers who were present in the service. God told him to minister differently, however, to three men who were present.

As Brother Hagin called those in fivefold ministry forward and began laying hands on them, the ushers were having difficulty moving quickly enough to keep up with Brother Hagin, so Ed jumped in to help the ushers catch the people as they were ministered to.

At one point, Brother Hagin grabbed Ed and said, "You

are one of the three I am to minister to differently." Then he put his arms around him and Ed felt something go into him as he fell to the floor under the power of the Spirit.

Ed received a mighty impartation that night into his life by the Spirit of God. From that time forward there has been an anointing upon Ed to minister to those with lumps and growths in their body.

In the many years of Ed's ministry since that time, there has been more healings of lumps and growths than of any other physical condition. Approximately 90 to 95 percent of all those ministered to have been healed.

How important it is for us and for those we are destined to minister to, that we receive all the impartations God would deposit in our lives.

What if Ed had not made the necessary sacrifices to be in that meeting? What if he had been too entangled with the daily demands of life to put spiritual things first? What if he had never received that impartation? Thousands of people who have been healed since that time would not have received healing through his ministry. We must always remember that our obedience or disobedience affects many people.

How many times have we had it in our hearts to attend a particular meeting, but something of such seemingly great importance arose at the last minute and prevented us from going? We must follow our hearts at all costs.

Someone may think, *Well, if I miss an impartation God has for me at one time, then He will cause me to receive it at a later time.*

You have no guarantee of that. The surest way to receive is to follow your heart and obey the Spirit's leading.

Romans 1:11 records what Paul wrote to the church in Rome, *"I long to SEE you, that I may impart unto you some spiritual gift, to the end ye may be established."*

Paul knew that some impartations could only take place when he "saw" them. You have to be in the presence of the man of God sometimes to receive all that God has for you. Books, tapes, and videos are a blessing, but they will never take the place of being in the presence of God's man when God has an impartation He wants to deposit into your life.

John Wesley's commentaries on the New Testament brought much clarity to Romans 1:11. *"I long to see you, that I may impart unto you some spiritual gift, to the end ye may be established."* Wesley stated that impartations come through preaching, teaching, private conversations, and the laying on of hands.

Throughout Ed's life many mighty men of God have laid hands on him and he has received great impartations. Through men's preaching and teaching he has received impartations; but also through private conversations he has received additional imparations.

Many times Ed has had the privilege of spending time listening to and asking questions of some of God's generals in private conversations. He has received many, many answers through the teachings and stories they have told him. How Ed loves their stories!

A Pastor's Pastor

Ed has received some mighty impartations through times of private conversations with Dr. Lester Sumrall.

Priceless was the time he was on the same flight as Dr. Sumrall and he pulled Ed up front to sit with him. "Sit next to me. I want to teach you how to cast out devils."

For hours Ed listened to God's general rehearse his many encounters of ministering to those demon-possessed and demon-oppressed in over a hundred nations of the world.

Just sitting in one of Dr. Sumrall's services, the spirit of boldness would come on you stronger. Just to have him lay his hands on you and bless you would rattle your bones!

Do whatever it takes to get around such God-filled men of your own company and let them speak into your life. It will cause your life, call, and ministry to be established.

Preaching Faith

Ed had been pastoring one of the first Word of Faith churches in the United States for only a short time when God began opening greater doors of ministry for him to travel in ministry.

He had been traveling frequently, but it was when Kenneth Copeland invited Ed, along with some other pastors, to come on his radio program, that many effectual doors for the traveling ministry were opened to him.

The Word of Faith message had begun to spread like wildfire and the teaching wave was gaining great momentum.

The topic discussed on a week of radio broadcasts by Kenneth Copeland and these pastors was, "Is It Possible to Pastor and Preach Faith?" Since God was bringing the message of faith to the forefront, that was a rather controversial topic. But now we see that not only is it possible to pastor and preach faith, but it's impossible to pastor without preaching faith!

Faith is the most important message in the Bible, for it's by grace that we are saved through faith. Without faith it's impossible to please God. The just shall live by faith. We walk by faith and not by sight. This is the victory that overcometh the world — even our faith. The life of the believer is governed by his faith.

The body of Christ needs to be proficient in operating in the principles of faith in order to live in the victory that is ours through Christ. It's imperative that pastors feed the sheep an on-going, healthy diet of faith principles.

When Jesus told Peter that Satan desired to have him to sift him like wheat, Jesus also let him know, *"But I have prayed for thee, that thy FAITH fail not. . ."* (Luke 22:32). Why did he pray for his faith? Satan was after his faith. Why? Because through faith, victories are wrought and Satan's defeat is enforced.

Hebrews 11:33 tells us, *"Who THROUGH FAITH subdued kingdoms, wrought righteousness, obtained promises. . . ."* Faith is the hand that takes what God has provided for His children.

Brother Hagin has stated that if he were to ever pastor again, he would designate one of his regular weekly services for teaching on faith or healing, for those are the two areas of greatest attack.

How important it is that we develop our faith, for then we live in the victory that is ours.

Chapter 15

Spiritual Fathers

As a young pastor, Ed had gotten hold of a book by Dr. Lester Sumrall titled, *Run with the Vision,* and was so stirred by it that he wanted to meet this man of bold, daring faith. It was while reading this book that God spoke to Ed, "I'm going to bring this man into your life."

Two weeks later, Ed was in the office when he received a phone call. "This is Lester Sumrall. I was told about your church and I want to come and preach for you!"

Ed was thrilled to finally have the opportunity to meet this man of God and have him in his church. Only weeks later Dr. Sumrall ministered at his church and the friendship they began to forge would last until the day Dr. Sumrall went home to be with the Lord.

Dr. Sumrall's life and message of faith left its mark on this young pastor, but it was the way Dr. Sumrall fathered and pastored him that made him so dear to Ed Dufresne.

No matter what Ed was facing, Dr. Sumrall was available to him to bring the pastoral advice that steadied him and gave him wisdom.

Although Ed had been in the ministry seventeen years by this time and had been married twenty-one years, recurring marriage problems came to a head and resulted in a divorce.

It was during this time of testing for Ed, his family, and his ministry, that Dr. Sumrall's fatherly wisdom and care became invaluable.

Shortly after Ed's divorce, Dr. Sumrall again preached at his church, but Ed was not in attendance at the service. When Ed returned to his office, there was Dr. Sumrall's business card slid beneath the glass on his desk with this message written on it,

> *Brother Ed, I deeply appreciate you. (Revelation 2:10). He who endures to the end shall possess all things.*
>
> *Don't QUIT! Don't slow down. Victory is sure, my friend. You are precious and I love you!*
>
> *Lester Sumrall*

As Ed read this love message from the hand of his dear pastor and spiritual father, he was fortified, loved, enriched, and ready to go forward.

Don't Go in Reverse

A short time later, as Ed's test blew on, he was in attendance at a convention where Dr. Sumrall preached. After the meeting, Dr. Sumrall approached Ed, "You're staying with me in the other bed in my hotel room tonight. When you wake up in the morning, you will be stronger! Strength will come into you!"

That night Dr. Sumrall sat in the hotel room across from Ed. "You can't go backwards, you can't go in reverse, or the devil will get you! There's no backing up — only going forward!"

These strong words of faith struck like arrows into Ed's heart and God's might within him increased. Strength, light, and life poured into him.

When they awoke the next morning, Dr. Sumrall left to get on his plane and Ed went back home, but now Ed was different! God's man had ministered to him, God's man had loved him, God's man had pastored him, God's man had encouraged him, and God's man had imparted into him.

There was no backing up. There was no going in reverse. To press on was the answer. Forward was the direction where God could be seen.

From that day forward, it was full speed ahead — right through barricades, hindrances, and all opposition. He had to go forward, for that's the direction of blessings. That's the direction heaven was pointing.

How crucial to the fulfilling of our calls and ministries, to have a spiritual father who speaks into our lives. Sometimes they bring correction or rebuke, as every good father will, but it's only to keep us safe and hold us in the place of great blessing.

If we stray from our spiritual fathers, we find ourselves lacking what only they can supply. How safe we are in the company of those whom God has anointed to be a fatherly voice into our lives. Let us not wander away from those whom God would use to parent us.

Brother Hagin opened his doors to Ed time and again and spoke into his life with words that hit their target.

Sitting across from Brother Hagin's desk, Ed would listen

to him share experiences of the past that would answer his questions and bring insight.

Brother Hagin would teach and train him in the things of the Spirit and in those things pertaining to the prophet's office.

But just as rich are the times when Ed attends Brother Hagin's meetings and has the edge of his anointing sharpened and his spirit fine-tuned to God's will.

Chapter 16

Quotes by
Dr. Lester Sumrall

We know you will be blessed to feast on the quotes of one of God's generals, Dr. Lester Sumrall.

- The love of the world is the barricade keeping Christians out of the supernatural.
- The secret to greatness is your decisions.
- God, help us to have enough sense to learn from those who have learned.
- All men of faith have feet of clay.
- You've got to keep your insides clean.
- If you don't conquer your insides, the devil will.
- Faith has no relationship with idleness. It always acts.
- The only way evil gets on top is for good to be on the bottom.
- Feed your faith and starve your doubts to death.
- Fear looks, faith jumps!
- Nothing I have done and nothing I'm doing is as great as what I'm going to do.
- Faith is knowing God.
- Other people's heads is no place for my joy.
- There's nothing greater than an idea whose time has come.

- There are four and a half billion people on the earth and they *are* your responsibility. (Todays estimate = 6 billion people.)
- Lord, don't do anything, what time I'm alive and me not be right in the middle of it.
- Make your obstacle a throne.
- Weeds grow quickly, but it takes time for flowers to bloom.
- At eighty-five give me a mountain full of giants and I'll slay them and fertilize the earth with their carcasses.
- The difference in people is between their ears.
- I don't do anything great – I just do something for God all the time.
- The universal approach to the human heart is the gospel.
- Never count yourself out of what God already counted you in on.
- Success is not success until you've created a successor.
- Anything great is related to suffering.
- You can't be defeated if you don't quit.
- God never expects faith beyond a man's experience.
- Any dedicated man is a misunderstood man.
- A man must have a cause before he will make an effect.
- Great causes are eternal.
- Retirement is of the devil.
- You make decisions and decisions make you.
- If you don't control your desires when you're young, they will control you when you're old.

Things that cause a minister to fall:
1. Don't think that you've ever arrived – possessions will make you think you've arrived. (Solomon's problem wasn't wealth, it was heaping it up for show.)
2. Don't plant worldly things in your mind.
3. Don't counsel the opposite sex.
4. Don't social drink.
5. Don't have too much free time.
6. Don't get a haughty spirit – don't be a know-it-all.
7. Don't be found with bad company.
8. Don't listen to your body.

Chapter 17

A New Direction

Although his family was going through great hardship as a result of the divorce, Ed was also concerned about the welfare of the sheep, for he knew that the repercussions from such a blow could be devastating to a congregation. So Ed stayed close to home and close to the sheep over the next year. The church continued to grow and experience God's blessing, and Ed continued to preach the uncompromising Word.

For the best interest of Ed's youngest daughter, God gave him a new direction. "Take your daughter and move to Tulsa, Oklahoma." With that word from God, Ed placed a pastor in the church and made the move to Tulsa.

Even while pastoring in Torrance, his schedule was full with traveling on almost a full-time basis, so with his ministry relocating to Oklahoma, he would concentrate solely on his traveling ministry.

Within a short time, the move was complete with a new home set up for his youngest daughter and himself, and new offices for the headquarters of his traveling ministry.

Chapter 18

God Is a Restorer

For more then twenty years, Ed had been believing God for a son named Stephen, but with the breakup of his marriage, that didn't seem to be a possibility anymore. So you can imagine his surprise, when in a meeting one night God spoke and said, "I'm going to give you a son named Stephen."

A few months later, God again spoke, "I'm going to give you a wife who plays the piano."

It had been two years now since Ed's divorce and he wanted to remarry. Many well-meaning friends and pastors had introduced him to some eligible girls in their congregations, but Ed began talking to God about sending him the wife of *His* choosing.

Where Do I Go from Here?

Although God had spoken to Ed about a wife and a son He would give him, I was a twenty-two-year-old single girl who had only been saved a short time and I had no idea I was soon to meet the man I would marry.

In 1984 I had just come out of a relationship that wasn't the will of God for me, and I was floundering to know God's plan for my life. So I set aside some extra time to just seek God concerning His will for my life.

I spent extra time reading my Bible and spent hours a day praying in other tongues. I wasn't fully aware at that time the great benefit I would derive from the extra amount of time spent praying in other tongues. I didn't even know that the passage in Romans 8:26,27 existed. I didn't know that when I prayed in tongues that I was praying according to the will of God for my life. I just knew that I had been out of the will of God for my life up to this time, and I didn't know what step to take next; but I did feel led to spend that extra time praying.

At the end of three weeks, I attended some church meetings with my brother, and it was at these meetings that I first met a man by the name of Ed Dufresne.

Ed, Nancy's Single Too!

The first night of meetings found my brother and me seated near the front of the sanctuary.

When it was time for the service to start, the minister walked through the side door by the platform and up to the pulpit. But another man followed him from the back room, whom I had never seen before, and took a seat on the front row.

The minister was a great blessing and the whole service was wonderful. When he finished teaching he called for those in the congregation who needed healing. As the front began to fill with those in the prayer line, the minister asked this other man, who had accompanied him from the back room, to join him in ministering to the sick.

He came forward and stood by the minister and they

began to lay hands on the sick.

They had ministered to only a few people when this fellow I was unacquainted with fell out on the floor as the power of God hit him.

He laid there for a few minutes unable to get up. With some help, he rose to his feet and returned to his seat on the front row.

At the close of the service, my brother and I walked out of the building and were headed toward my car in the parking lot.

It was raining outside so we were moving quickly to reach the car.

A gentleman I knew called after us from the front door. "Nancy, would you and your brother like to come in the back room and then go with the ministers to the restaurant?"

"Sure," my brother and I agreed. "Thank you."

So we made our way back into the building and followed him into the back room where the ministers were gathered.

My brother and I stepped into the hospitality room, noticing the handful of people present.

I was friends with the wife of the minister who had conducted the service, and she noticed my brother and me as soon as we stepped in the door. "Oh Ed," she exclaimed, "Nancy's single too!"

This dear lady is precious to me, but I will have to admit that I was caught by surprise and a little bit embarrassed.

So this was my formal introduction to the man I was soon to marry.

I think he was as embarrassed as I was, but I will never forget seeing this man up close for the first time, as he sat on the top of a high counter with his legs swinging down the front of the cabinet doors.

We politely exchanged glances and smiled, hoping the attention would soon turn from us.

So What Are You Called To Do?

A few moments later, we were out the door and following the others to the nearby Denny's restaurant, which was the only place that stayed open late.

As we made our way inside and to the table, the minister's wife directed everyone where to sit.

"Ed, you sit here," as she pointed to a chair on the end.

"Nancy, you sit here next to Ed." I slid into the chair beside him without another thought about it.

Ed and the minister began talking about the things of God and I thoroughly enjoyed hearing them discuss God's Word. Although there were about ten people at the table, the attention was focused on listening to these two ministers.

I had never been in a setting like that before and it was a real blessing.

Ed hadn't spoken to me while at the restaurant, but I didn't think much about it since it never dawned on me that we would ever develop any kind of relationship.

We went through the entire dinner without saying anything to each other; and it wasn't until after everyone had finished eating that Ed turned to me and asked, "So, what has God called you to do?"

With my life having been in a state of turmoil for the past months and being so uncertain of my future, that was one question that was too big for me to answer at that moment. I just mumbled something quickly to get the conversation turned away from me.

Although Ed had shown little interest in striking up a conversation, he was polite but aloof.

He later explained that every time he would show interest in starting a relationship with someone, God would tell him, "No, she's not the one for you." So when we met, he assumed God would again say the same thing. Therefore, Ed's thought was, *Why even bother!*

The evening came to an uneventful close, as everyone said their "good nights," then my brother and I went back to my apartment.

We Meet Again

The following evening found us again seated toward the front for the second and final night of services.

Ed once again attended the meetings and assisted his minister friend in ministering to the sick.

It was a wonderful service with a lot of people being ministered to, and as it ended, my brother and I again made our way to my car to leave.

A replay of the previous evening took place and we

were again invited to the minister's room, after which we all gathered again at the same Denny's restaurant.

The Trap Is Laid

As we arrived at the restaurant, everyone was mingling around the table before anyone was seated.

At this point, Ed and I had only politely exchanged greetings, but there was certainly no indication on either of our parts that there would soon be a budding romance.

Before sitting down, the minister's wife approached me. "Nancy, what is your phone number? Ed really likes you and wants to have your number."

I never could have been more shocked to hear her statement. As we say in Oklahoma, "You could have knocked me over with a feather!"

"You mean that man I sat by last night?" I asked in amazement. "Why, he hardly even spoke to me!"

"Well, don't you like him?" she prodded.

"I have no idea! I don't even know him!"

"Well, give me your phone number and then he can call you," she urged.

Since I was planning to visit my sister in Texas the very next week, I got a small piece of paper and jotted down her number to give to the minister's wife.

I never really thought he would ever call me, so I didn't give it much more thought.

With paper in hand, the minister's wife marched right over to Ed and, unknown to me, pushed it into Ed's hand. "Ed,

Nancy really likes you and wants you to have her phone number. So call her."

The trap had been laid!

He was probably just as shocked to get my phone number as I was when she asked me for it.

He didn't really consider me to be his type, so he just shoved the piece of paper in his suit pocket.

He acted a little more warmly toward me that evening, but I probably acted the same way toward him too.

Another Encounter

The next day, the minister's wife began calling me. "Jerry Savelle just gave Ed his plane and we're going to fly with Ed to his next meeting. We're just going to fly up there and back the same night, so why don't you go with us?" she invited.

"Well, I don't know. Since it's Ed's plane, shouldn't he be the one inviting me?" I questioned.

"He said it's all right if you come with us," she reassured me.

I replied, "Well, I feel a little uncomfortable about it." I didn't want Ed to feel obligated to let me come along just because our minister friends had asked me.

Ed was certainly a nice man, but I still wasn't convinced that he had any real interest toward me, and I didn't want him to feel that I was pursuing him.

I knew that he would be considered a "good catch" by any single Christian woman; and the last thing I wanted to do was make him feel like he was being cornered by "another admiring female." Besides, having just come out of a relationship, I wasn't sure about getting into a dating situation so soon.

"Why don't the four of us go out to lunch this week?" my friend suggested, "then at the lunch he can invite you on the trip himself."

"Well, that would be okay" I agreed, "but I leave on Saturday to visit my sister, so it will have to be before then."

"Okay, I'll call you back and let you know when and where."

My friend called back confirming that the three of them would meet me on Friday at a Chinese restaurant for lunch.

Before Friday arrived, my friend and I spoke on the phone several times, mainly discussing Ed and his ministry. They had been friends for several years, so it was nice to know a little bit about him and his ministry.

My friend, in turn, would call Ed and they would discuss me.

Oh, the joys of being single! There's nothing like the dating scene to totally keep you guessing. Thank God I'm redeemed!

Friday finally arrived and we all met for our scheduled lunch date.

Ed and the minister had a nice time of fellowship, and my friend and I had a good time talking, but again, few words were exchanged between Ed and me. (To hear Ed tell his side of the story, he says that he didn't even know that I was to be having lunch with them, so he was shocked to see me arrive with them.)

It seemed a little strained and I felt self-conscious.

Knowing that there was twenty years difference between Ed and me, I didn't want to say something stupid that made me sound immature, so I was more quiet than usual.

During the course of lunch, Ed did invite me to make the trip with them in his new plane if I wanted to, but I certainly didn't read it as him setting up another date to see me.

What a Beautiful Home

After lunch we all rode in one car, leaving my car at the restaurant to get a tour of Ed's new house.

It was a large, beautiful home that his oldest daughter, Carole, had just decorated, and it was located on a wooded lot.

He had all new furniture and everything was in place. The pictures and flower arrangements were lovely and I was awed by the size of the home and its beauty. I hadn't been in too many homes that looked like this and it was quite a treat for me.

When we made our way down from the upstairs, I noticed a lovely, large grandfather clock with inlaid wood. I stopped to admire it and when I did, I noticed something in Ed sparked.

He told me all about the clock and it seemed to open up our conversation with one another.

When we walked into the living room, Ed introduced me to his fifteen-year old daughter Stephanie, who was sitting in a white armed chair in front of the large living room windows.

She was just beautiful and seemed a little timid, as a lot of fifteen-year olds are when parents invade their home with a group of gawking adults.

She greeted us sweetly and the five of us stood there for a while making small talk before heading out the door.

As we walked outside, we stood in the driveway and my friend set us up, "Ed, we need to go. Why don't you drive back to the restaurant to pick up Nancy's car?" How convenient!

So, we climbed into his brand new 1984 Jeep Wrangler and headed back toward the restaurant.

We had a nice, casual conversation on the ride back, but still, no romance sparks flew for either one of us.

Who's Jack Harper?

The next day I loaded the luggage into my car and headed to Texas to visit my sister and her family.

I had been there about a week when I received a phone call. My sister called me to the phone, "Nancy, there's a guy by the name of Jack Harper on the phone for you."

Jack Harper, I wondered, *Who's Jack Harper?*

"Hello?"

The voice on the other end of the phone began, "This is Jack Harper. Do you remember me?"

My mind raced. Jack Harper. Jack Harper. I didn't re-member anyone by that name.

Having given up my title as Miss Oklahoma almost a year before, I wondered if it was someone I had met during my reign. No, I had no idea who this was.

"I'm sorry, but you're going to have to refresh my memory," I answered half embarrassed.

The man on the other end talked for a moment then confessed, "No, this is Ed Dufresne."

Now I was surprised! It never dawned on me that he would be calling, but we had a wonderful conversation that lasted almost an hour.

Ma Bell, Our Friend

For the next several days he continued to call, sometimes two and three times a day. For some reason we communicated so much better on the phone than we did in person and we were beginning to get to know one another.

Little did we know at that time that Ma Bell would play a major role in our relationship and marriage. We have kept the phone company prosperous ever since that day, but it has been worth every dime.

I recall Dad Hagin telling how he and Mom Hagin wrote love letters to each other every day while he was away from home on his many preaching tours. They would fill the pages telling each other of their events of the day. It kept their marriage tender and their love flourishing.

What letters were for Dad and Mom Hagin, the telephone was for our budding relationship.

Not only was Ed calling, but the minister's wife was also calling and urging our relationship on. She was very involved with what was transpiring between Ed and me and she actually was very instrumental in getting us together.

Ed was being cautious for his own reasons, and I was being cautious for my own reasons. But she kept us from being so cautious that we wouldn't follow our hearts.

A Fitting Story

"Do you know what made me decide to start calling you?" Ed asked.

"No, what?"

"While in my meetings this week in California, I put my hand in my suit pocket and found your phone number that was given to me while we were at Denny's.

"I wondered whether or not I should call you and decided against it. I thought the age difference would be an issue for you.

"But while I was at dinner with some ministers after my meeting, a dear woman of God said to me, 'Ed, I want to tell you a story.' Without her knowing anything about us, she told me of a relative of hers whose spouse was thirty years younger; she told me all about their wonderful marriage and how madly in love they always were with each other.

"When she told me that story," Ed continued, "I knew then that our age difference didn't have to be a problem."

How faithful God is to cause us to hear a right word in due season. All of these events are precious little nuggets in our lives that Ed and I cherish, for they testify of God's guiding hand that brought us together.

It's My Birthday

On Friday, June 9th, I again received a call from Ed Dufresne, alias Jack Harper. "Tomorrow is my birthday, so what do you think about me flying down to Texas in the morning and us spending the day together?"

I was a little taken back to think that a man would fly to where I was so we could be together, so I hesitated.

I so enjoyed talking to him on the phone, but when we were together in person, we didn't seem to communicate too well. What if he flew here and the same thing happened again?

I thought the safest thing to do for both of us would be to just wait until I returned to Tulsa.

"On Sunday I am planning to drive back to Tulsa, so maybe we can just get together sometime next week," I suggested.

"Are you sure? I don't have anything planned for my birthday."

"Oh, I don't want you to go to the trouble and expense. I'll just see you next week," I reassured him.

After hanging up the phone, I got ready to go play tennis with my brother-in-law. On the way out the door I instructed my sister, "When Ed calls back in a few minutes and tells you he's flying down here in the morning, come and get me at the tennis court."

Then I stopped. "Why did I say that?" I wondered. "He's not going to come here."

Without another thought about it, I headed out the door.

My brother-in-law and I had been playing tennis for about five minutes when my sister drove up. "Ed just called back and said he'll be here in the morning. Come on home, we've got to clean house!"

We hurried to get the house in order that evening, then I made an Italian creme cake for Ed's birthday.

A Date with Jack Harper

The next morning my sister, my brother-in-law, and I drove to the airport. As we stood at the end of the jetway waiting for Ed to exit I held a sign, "Jack Harper."

I thought he would get a chuckle out of it, but he acted like he didn't see it and walked right past us.

I knew right then that we were going to get along just fine!

That afternoon we went back to the house and the four of us had a good time playing a game of croquet in the backyard and sitting on the back porch.

That evening we all went to dinner and then a movie. We finally returned to the house to have some birthday cake.

Ed and I spent the remainder of the evening in that little, quiet, country town sitting on the back porch, talking.

Healing Power

At one point I walked over to the edge of the porch and looked out over the backyard.

Ed came up behind me and placed his hand on my back. "God's healing your back. Did you know that the devil planned for you to be in a wheelchair within ten years?"

I hadn't told this man that I had suffered with extreme

back trouble for several years. I knew it was God who had revealed it to him.

I had suffered with severe headaches and had bouts with my back when I was virtually unable to get up or down without extreme pain. There were times when I had struggled to get in and out of cars because the pain was so severe.

What kind of man was this? I had never been around someone so full of God.

I had only been saved two and a half years and was still so young in spiritual things, but this man walked with God in a way that I was hungry for.

Spiritual Growth

One of the things that I have always admired about Ed is how he never looked down on my lack of spiritual maturity. Although he had been in the ministry for over twenty years at the time we met, he never once made me feel as if I was beneath him in spiritual things. He never made me feel as if what I had to say was insignificant or unimportant.

Many has been the time when I said the wrong thing, but he never scolded me. He just let me grow out of it.

When some single people set their ideas of what they're looking for in a mate, they decide that they won't even consider someone who hasn't attained to a certain spiritual level. But that isn't right. If someone is hungry for God, they will grow.

When believing God for the right spouse, believers should only marry someone who is saved. But you don't necessarily look for someone who has achieved a certain level of spirituality. Rather, look for someone who is hungry for God, for that's the one who will grow in God, no matter what level of spiritual growth they are currently at.

My Bible School

Although I was spiritually young, Ed saw the hunger in my heart for God and he knew that the maturity would follow.

After we were married and I first heard Ed preach, I was so young in the Lord that I didn't even understand what he meant when he made reference to the fivefold ministry. Having been raised in a Methodist church, the pastor was the only fivefold office we ever knew anything about.

But as I sat under Ed's ministry, I began to grow by leaps and bounds spiritually. He became my Bible school and I was learning more than I had ever learned before.

One thing that God had me do, as a student of Ed's ministry, was to keep a journal of all of Ed's meetings that I attended. I recorded outlines of his sermons, any prophecies that he gave, and the healings that took place. In essence, God had me write one of my own textbooks.

Whenever we would go back to the hotel room following the service, Ed would tell me different things he knew by the Spirit and I would record these as well. By doing this, I was able to learn more about the moving of the Holy Spirit and the operations of God.

After we were married, one of the things that I battled was wondering why God did not have Ed marry someone who was seasoned in ministry. *Someone like that,* I thought, *would have been of greater help to Ed in his services and ministry.*

But God made it clear to my heart that he wanted someone who could be raised up under Ed and trained to flow in a way that enhanced his ministry.

Heading Home

The following morning Ed and I loaded up my brand new two-seater Fiero and headed back towards Tulsa on a drive that would take us eight hours to complete.

As we neared Tulsa, I began getting a sinking feeling on the inside and I didn't know why until I realized that it was because our weekend together was coming to an end.

It was on Sunday that we made our drive back to Tulsa, but I was thankful when Ed asked me out to dinner for the following Tuesday evening. Even though I knew I would be with him again in a couple of days, I still felt empty just knowing I was getting ready to drop him off at his own home.

These feelings were most unexpected for me, but I didn't dare let him know what I was feeling. I dropped him off at his house and headed back to my apartment.

I dropped my luggage in my bedroom just in time to answer the ringing phone.

"Hello?"

"How about if I come and get you and we go get some ice cream?" I was thrilled to hear Ed's voice, and the lonely feeling quickly disappeared. It was surprising to me that he seemed to want to be with me as much as I wanted to be with him. So, we spent our Sunday evening continuing to get to know one another as we enjoyed our ice cream.

Around midnight, he returned me back to my apartment and went home. A few minutes later the phone rang again. I answered it to find Ed on the other end and we talked until about 3:00 a.m. (Now that we are married, I realize what a big sacrifice he made in staying up that late, for his schedule is so demanding).

We didn't wait until our Tuesday night date to be together, for on Monday we again found time to go out for ice cream, then we spent a good portion of the night on the phone together.

Get in or Get Out!

On Tuesday evening we went out and had a wonderful dinner together at a beautiful restaurant, then went back to his house and watched television. It was while at his house that he turned to me and said, "I'm falling in love with you and if you don't feel the same way, we need to get out of this relationship. I'm too old to be playing a dating game, so if this isn't what you want, we need to end it."

I was dumbfounded! None of our conversations had carried such a serious tone nor had we even expressed the idea of being in love with each other.

I had been cautious against letting my thoughts turn so serious, especially since I had just come out of a relationship only a short time before.

I certainly don't mean to sound as if I was not interested

in our relationship becoming so serious, but I never dreamed it would advance so quickly. I expected that he would want to move slowly and be very cautious about becoming seriously involved with someone too quickly.

When Ed stated that he was falling in love with me, and that if I didn't feel the same way that we needed to end the relationship, I didn't know what to say. I loved being with him, but I didn't know what I thought since everything had moved so quickly — I didn't know what to say or how I felt, so I just got real quiet. He must have noticed it, for he quickly became quiet too and we put a quick end to the evening.

He's Going To Be Your Husband!

The next day, which was Wednesday, I was driving down the street in Tulsa and began talking to God about my relationship with Ed. "Father, I can't believe that I have gotten myself in this relationship. I just got out of that other relationship and have been restored into right fellowship with You, but I don't know what to do about this situation! If this isn't the one, tell me how to get out of it."

"He's going to be your husband!" The words resounded so big that it seemed to me like an audible voice spoke in the car. When God spoke those words to me, I was instantly in love with him. Those words not only brought God's will to my understanding, but a deep love for Ed was put in me.

Up until this time, I had loved being with him, but now I was in love with him and it was different — I knew it was the will of God.

Let's Get a Ring

Since the previous night had ended on a rather strained note, I wasn't sure what Ed's response to me would be on Wednesday evening. He was scheduled to leave for a ten-day preaching tour in Europe on Thursday, so he asked me to come to his house while he packed.

Thankfully there seemed to be none of the strain of the previous night when I got to his house. We talked while he packed, but I never mentioned to him what God had said to me that day while in my car.

But Ed would still surprise me further. "When I get back from Germany, I'm going to buy you a ring!" This time I had heard from God and I agreed wholeheartedly.

"I'll call you every day," Ed promised as he left for Germany on Thursday morning. We did talk to each other on the phone while he was in Germany — for at least two hours a day! He paid quite a hefty phone bill when he got back but he insists it was a good investment.

I learned early on, that although times of separation from Ed were never easy, to be thankful that God even enlists us in His service and allows us to work with Him in whatever way He chooses, giving us all the grace we need.

We're Getting Married

While Ed was in Germany the conversation changed from, "When I get home I'm gonna buy you a ring!" to "When I get home, we're getting married!" His ten-day tour was shortened to nine days and I was so excited to meet him at the airport upon his return home.

Within a few days of Ed's return from Germany, we eloped. Our minister friends, who introduced us, performed the intimate ceremony at their home, and then we boarded Ed's new plane and were off on a day and a half honeymoon. We had only told a few people of our intentions to marry and we felt it best to elope rather than have a big wedding. It turned out that elopement was the best route.

We were so happy and thankful for God's restoring hand working in both of our lives.

After our short honeymoon we were off together, on the road ministering and having the time of our lives.

There was much for me to learn about this wonderful man and God's plan for our lives, but what a thrill it has been!

It's the Exception, Not the Rule

The way God brought us together was very unique and is the exception, not the rule. Few are the times that God will ever lead a couple to get married so soon after having met, and rarely does a quick-decision marriage work, but for our lives, it was His will.

Before we even met, Ed had been praying regarding a wife and I had spent a considerable time waiting before the Lord to know His will.

We had both decided that we weren't going to become willful and pick who we wanted to marry, but we were going to let God put it together. That's why we were able to get God's best. We took the time to wait before God so we would know His will.

If you're believing God for a spouse, just rest in His ability to bring you the right one. Don't go out and pick someone yourself, but let *Him* do the choosing. The one He chooses for you will make you happy beyond your wildest dreams.

But it doesn't stop there! Treat your spouse like you would treat Jesus and your marriage will be heavenly. Put your spouse first at all times and you will have a sweet marriage. Walk in love at all times, never doing anything selfishly and the rewards will be rich.

Heaven on Earth

Marriage for us has been like heaven on earth. No doubt, Ed has had to overlook a lot of ignorance and immaturity on my part concerning life and ministry, but he has always dealt with me in a most gracious, patient, and loving way.

Our schedule and lives were full as we traveled together. God's blessing and anointing on Ed's life continued to increase and I was learning so much.

But change for our lives wasn't to stop there. After being married only a few weeks, I became pregnant with our first child. You may think it was sudden, as I undoubtedly thought, but when you consider the fact that Ed had been believing for a son for twenty years, I guess you couldn't call it sudden. So in 1985, Stephen was born and our family grew.

Chapter 19

Will You Do Me a Favor?

In 1986 Ed began conducting Sunday afternoon miracle services in a little town on the outskirts of Tulsa called Jenks, Oklahoma. After several months, we began construction of our new ministry headquarters and auditorium in Jenks, Oklahoma. Miracle services and special meetings were conducted there, as well as regular church services.

Ed had been conducting services there for three years, and in 1989 when Ed stepped onto the platform one Sunday morning, he heard another sound from heaven.

"Will you do Me a favor?" came the question from God as Ed mounted the platform steps.

"You know I will. What is it?" came Ed's quick response.

"I want you to move back to California and get into position for what I'm going to do on earth during the last days."

Ed had not thought of returning to California. So much had transpired since the last time he lived there, but he knew that if he was to be in God's perfect will, it would mean returning to his home state. We wanted to be in the position where God wanted us.

We both knew it was God's will to move back to California. Ed had it all figured out how it was to take place. He would put the building on the market, along with the

115

eighty-five adjoining acres we owned; we would take the cash from the sale of the building and property, relocate our headquarters to Southern California, and begin anew in the place where God was directing us to go.

Start Packing

A year and a half later, no one had made a cash offer on the building and property, as we expected. We decided that we had been in Oklahoma long enough waiting for the sale.

Ed marched into the offices one day and said, "God spoke to me. What would we do if we had a buyer for the building and property? We would pack up, right?"

"Sure," the staff agreed.

"Well then," instructed Ed, "start packing! Faith is an act and we know that God wants us in California and we know that it's time for us to go there. We're going to go as far as we can toward making the move on our part, then God will meet us, supplying His part."

So, the packing began! Records, files, and furniture were packed away into boxes — only what was needed to operate was left in place.

As the last office was packed up, we received an offer on the building and we were on our way to California.

Going "Not Knowing"

We learned again that we have to go "not knowing," for the man of faith always goes forward "not knowing." We started packing "not knowing" about a buyer. We knew God spoke, we knew it was time, but we didn't know everything about the steps to come. As we took the steps we did know — packing up the building — God showed us the next steps to take.

In Acts 20:22 Paul tells us, *"And now, behold, I go bound in the spirit unto Jerusalem, NOT KNOWING the things that shall befall me there."*

Paul knew he was to go to Jerusalem. He knew it was time, but he didn't know everything that was to come. The man of faith doesn't get disturbed about going "not knowing," because he's following the One who does know, and that's enough for him.

Smith Wigglesworth, a preacher from England, made this statement, "The secret of power is going without knowing."

Hebrews 11:8 in *The Amplified Bible* reads, *"[Urged on] by faith Abraham, when he was called, obeyed and went forth to a place which he was destined to receive as an inheritance; and he went, although HE DID NOT KNOW OR TROUBLE HIS MIND ABOUT WHERE HE WAS TO GO."*

There are times we can get into some difficulty if we prematurely try to step into something that God has put in our hearts, for knowing the timing of God is just as important as knowing the plan of God. We must be sure it is His timing we are following. But when it's time to move, we can be assured that the "not knowing" path is the one we are to take.

The Hebrews were led out of Egypt with Moses at the helm "not knowing" where they would find food, water, and home, but God was leading them. In fact, one of the first places He led them was to the banks of the Red Sea, hemmed in by mountains on either side, and an enemy army behind them. God led them to the place where they would need a miracle. God led them to the place where He was their only defense. He was their great Waymaker!

We made the move to Southern California in 1990 and began immediately securing headquarters for the ministry. We rented a home and began settling in to our new surroundings.

We saw God's hand of blessing move many times in preparing a way for us.

World Harvest Church

In 1991, a year after we had moved to California, God spoke to Ed about starting a church. I was to pastor it and Ed was to continue to travel. How beautifully this has worked for us and we are so happy to be able to serve God in whatever way pleases Him.

We dearly love our church family and look forward to all that God has planned for us as a congregation.

A Place to Call Home

We had lived in California for about two years when Ed came downstairs announcing, "God told me that it's time for us to buy a home." I handled our personal finances, and although we were doing fine financially, I knew that in the natural, we didn't have all we needed in the bank to purchase a home. But I knew this -- it didn't matter! Since God had said that it was time to purchase a home, we would have all that we needed.

That day Ed began driving around the area and returned in a few hours with the glad announcement, "I found it!"

He took me to see this beautiful home on some acreage and we agreed — this was it! He began taking steps to see what it would take to purchase it. After a few days, Ed gave the update.

"Two brothers own the house. They had it built two years ago (which is when we moved back to California) and it has not been lived in since it was built. I made them an offer and they were discussing the offer in front of their mother. She heard them say that a preacher wanted to buy the home. "What's the preacher's name?" she asked her sons.

"Ed Dufresne."

"I was healed in one of his meetings years ago in Torrance, California. Sell him the house and give him a good deal!"

Thank God for mamas! They did sell it to us and God made a way where there was seemingly no way. The care He gives His own children is masterful and loving. How safe we are in His care!

A Growing Family

In 1994 our family grew again to include our second son, Grant Wesley Dufresne, born on April 20.

It's a thrill to be able to raise our sons around the things of God, and we look forward to serving God together with them.

Chapter 20
Spiritual Happenings

"Tell Them She's with Me"

There's always a purpose in any manifestation from heaven. God is the God of all comfort and many times, great comfort has come from heaven's manifestations. One such message of comfort came during one of Ed's services.

A minister and his wife were present in the service who had recently experienced the tragedy of their daughter's suicide. Before her death she had received Christ, but her mind was weak and shortly after her conversion she took her own life.

Since her death, the devil had tormented this girl's mother with the thought that her daughter had gone to hell because she committed suicide.

However, a person can be sick in their mind just like they can be sick in their body. People who die with mental illness are no more likely to go to hell because of it any more than someone who dies as the result of a physical illness.

In the middle of Ed's service, he saw Jesus appear in midair, just in front of the balcony. On one side of Jesus stood Ed's own mother. Although she had died at the age of forty-five of alcoholism, she received Jesus the night before her death.

As she stood beside Jesus in this vision, Ed marveled at how young and joyful she looked.

But standing on the other side of Jesus was a girl who looked to be in her twenties, whom Ed had never seen before.

"Jesus, who is that young girl standing with You?" Ed asked.

"This is C's_____ daughter. You tell C _____ that her daughter is with Me," came Jesus' reply.

As Ed told the mother about her daughter he saw standing beside Jesus, they rejoiced and wept with joy as the cloud of torment lifted. Ed told them how beautiful, peaceful, and joyful she looked.

How wonderful is the comfort that God gives.

Heaven is so near. Our loved ones who have relocated to heaven are living in a place that is so close and dear. We have not lost them. One day soon we will rejoice with them again. Oh yes, we miss their presence here with us, but we can rejoice knowing they are with the Lord.

One Hundred Healing Angels

In the early 1980's, as Ed was coming off a plane and exiting off the jetway, the Spirit of God spoke to him, "Turn around." As he did, he saw a hundred angels following him, standing in a line, two abreast. "These are one hundred healing angels being dispatched to work with you in the healing ministry."

Do we find any record of angels who operate in this

manner in the Bible? In John 5:2-4 we read of the five porches full of impotent folk, blind, halt, withered, and lame who lay by the pool of Bethesda, waiting for the moving of the water. At a certain season an angel would go down into the pool and stir the water; the first one into the water was healed. The angel worked on heaven's behalf to deposit healing power into the water.

During the meetings, Ed will sometimes see angels working on a person's back or bringing new body parts from heaven, such as heart valves or other internal organs needed by the people. There have been times when the congregation has seen a person move in a way physically impossible while an angel worked on their afflicted body area.

Other people have testified to feeling body parts move within their bodies, or tell of feeling a hand reach inside their body and move internal organs around.

We don't worship angels or focus our attention on them, but we do acknowledge that they are heaven's messengers and we are to receive what they bring us from our homeland.

We don't seek to make these things happen, for they happen as the Spirit wills. These incidents are prevalent in the life and ministry of Ed Dufresne because of the prophet's anointing that is upon his life.

Our place, as members of the body of Christ, is to receive what the true prophets see and hear from heaven and as we do, we are blessed by what God reveals to them. *"Believe his prophets, so shall ye prosper"* (2 Chronicles 20:20).

A Talking Fetus

Only a few years after we were married, we had gone to bed and I was beginning to fall asleep when Ed nudged me. "I'm having a vision, get a pen and paper and write down what I tell you. I'm seeing a fetus and it's talking to me, saying, 'One day when you get to heaven I will thank you and your partners for letting me live on the earth.'"

We have many things in our hearts for ministry to babies and children, and the fullness of God's plan will come to pass in His time.

Hanging from a Satellite

In the earlier years of his ministry, Ed had a vision that has yet to come to pass, but it has continued to stir in his heart. He saw himself hanging off a satellite and declaring, "Jesus is the Healer!" We know that this vision is for an appointed time.

Healing Anointing Increases

Years ago God told Ed, "When you stand in the full measure of the prophet's anointing, even cancer won't be able to stand before that anointing."

Multiple cancer victims, who were given only days to live, have been healed in Ed's ministry, and the number of those healings continues to increase.

Chapter 21

Before the Throne

"And immediately I was in the spirit: and, behold, a throne was set in heaven, and one sat on the throne"

(Revelation 4:2).

In October 1999, Ed had an encounter with God like he had never experienced before. We were leaving a service in Oakland, California, that had been marked by some outstanding healings and a mighty move of the Spirit.

As Ed was exiting the auditorium and standing in the hallway, those of us with him heard him say, "Lord, I don't know if I can go out that far." Then he fell against the wall and down to the floor. As he lay there we heard him say, "Jesus, I'm not worthy to see Your face," and then he began repenting.

Those of us around him heard him say, "Yes, the buildings will come up, the ministry will come up. This is the time I've been waiting for. Cancers will be healed." With that he rose to his feet and told us what happened.

As he exited the building, he saw outer space and heaven beyond that. That's when we heard him say, "Lord, I don't know if I can go that far." At that point, God took him out of his body, he fell against the wall, then down to the floor. He was carried to the throne room of God and was bowed down before God's throne. All he saw of God was His legs and feet

125

— so awesome was the sight that words can't fully describe the scene.

As he was prostrate before God's throne, those of us gathered heard Ed say, "I'm not worthy."

Throughout Ed's years of ministry he has boldly preached that Jesus has made us righteous and we are worthy because of what He did for us; but Ed said that when he was before God's throne, the awesomeness of it was so astounding that he forgot all of that.

Thank God, Jesus has made us righteous so that we can come boldly before the throne of grace and obtain that which we need. (2 Corinthians 5:21, Hebrews 4:16.)

While he was before God's throne, other things were spoken to him; he then felt someone touch his head. He didn't know whether it was God, Jesus, or an angel who touched him. It seemed to Ed that he was touched with miracle power. Since then the anointing has increased and God told him that he had entered into the full measure of the prophet's anointing.

I Am Determined!

The preparations made in a man's life for ministry determine the outreach of his ministry, and as Dad Hagin has taught us, "Preparation time is never lost time."

With thirty-five years of training, preparation, and impartations, we see into the life of Ed Dufresne, a man who is spiritually dressed to win his race.

So what lies ahead? Ed Dufresne will be running with the momentum of thirty-five years of preparation propelling him forward so that he will run to carry God's healing power to this generation.

The will of God for this ministry will come to pass!

How do we know? Because Ed has declared, "I am determined!"

Part II
Visions and Prophecies for the Body of Christ

Given by Dr. Ed Dufresne

"Get in the River" Vision
Fresh Oil Conference - May 5, 1997
World Harvest Church
Murrieta, California

God gave me this mini vision a year ago last New Year's concerning this coming revival. I was standing in the middle of a dry riverbed. I was standing there and I looked up and here was this boat sitting in the dry riverbed. There were people in this boat, and God said, "Now this boat represents the church of this certain group. They're stuck in a dry riverbed."

The people were in there and they were rowing. They were sweating. They were just trying to pull the oars and as they were pulling these oars, dust was flying up from the sand. The oars were going in the sand. I said, "My goodness, they don't even know there's no water in that riverbed! They don't even know it!" They're saying, "Isn't this great? The seventies and eighties sure have been great." And here there's that dust flying up. Then a man stood up and God said, "This is the pastor of this church," and he opened his mouth and a puff of dust came out. I said, "My God, he doesn't even know he's dry." The people are deceived. They're in there rowing and working and sweating and they're trying to get that boat to move and it isn't moving because there's no water in the river."

All of a sudden I heard a bunch of shouting. There was a levee and here came this river and God said, "This is the revival of today." I heard these people screaming and yelling and laughing and shouting and I noticed that they weren't rowing. Their oars were laid inside in the bottom of the boat and they had their hands raised just praising and shouting. God said, "Those that go with this river won't even have to toil. They won't even have to work. They're just in the river." The name of the church, "Whosoever Is Hungry and Thirsty," was on the boat. They stood up and they were loud. They were shouting and dancing and full of joy and then a man stood up and God said, "This is the pastor of this new church," and he opened his mouth and fire shot out of his mouth.

Whoever is thirsty can get in this boat. It didn't have any movement name. It didn't have any denominational name. It was going over those barriers.

They said, "This is wonderful. All our needs are met. Did you see that miracle? Did you see that one raised from the dead? Did you see that word of knowledge? Did you see the gifts of faith in operation? The gifts of healing? Working of miracles? The word of knowledge that prophet walked in?"

The prophet's office will be revived as it was in the day when they walked under that heavy anointing. I said, "Lord, I'm going to get in the middle of that boat." He said, "Well, you rowed ten years ago – that's part of what I was showing you in *Fresh Oil* when you wrote the book ten years ago. This revival is the Word and the Spirit. This way you won't get off into the ditch, the dry riverbed. In this river all our needs will be met. It won't be a struggle. It won't be by might. It was by the river which represents the Holy Ghost and the anointing. The anointing will bring the mountains down when you're in that flow, that river. This revival is going to go over the banks and it's going to flood everything."

Fresh Oil Conference - May 5, 1997
World Harvest Church
Murrieta, California

This anointing, this river that is flowing right now, those that jump into this river are going to revive. In other words, restoration. Restoration of the gifts of the Spirit, restoration of those that have been dead.

Those who fought in World War II and that were in fox-holes and gave their hearts to the Lord, a lot of them are dead, but there are still a remnant in this planet earth. They cried out to God. In My mercy this anointing is going to hit the back-slider and they're going to come running to the church. It's already started.

Those who were in the foxholes of Vietnam who cried out to God, "God, save me." Bullets flying all over. Mortars flying all over. Crying out, "Mama, or God, whoever can help me right now. . . ." God was there and saved them and helped them get out of there and they came back to the United States and got discouraged and they ran from God and they did all kinds of things. They're coming to the church. They're coming to the church. This river's going to hit them and they're going to be revived, and the dead men are going to stand up on their feet and they're going to be hot for God. They're going to come running.

The buildings won't be big enough with this river. This river, this anointing that we're in right now, is going to revive the backslider and they're going to come. You're going to see the bikers. You're going to see homosexuals crying out, "God, get me free of this!" And that river, they're going to get caught up in that anointing, and they're going to stand up on their feet and come back to God! Kids that have run from home and that have run from God, preachers' kids that have run because they saw their mother and dad being persecuted, they're going to run back to the church, on fire for God. Believe ye the prophets. They're coming. Souls are coming. The backsliders are coming back to God.

The anointing of God's moving on this earth, because the anointing has a job description to destroy yokes. You're to get tanked up and then go out there and get them.

Things are being revived. Strength's being revived. Our bodies are being revived. When we get in this anointing, then we can run faster than ever, but smarter.

What happened to those cots? What happened to those ambulances when they used to come to the Church and back up at the back door and carry those who were dying with needles in them? They're coming. They're going to be revived. They're going to start coming to the churches that are in the river, in the anointing that revives.

Ain't going to be by your program. Ain't going to be because you're an eloquent speaker and you're so smart. Ain't going to happen. And no denomination's going to get the glory for this one. They're not going to put their vise grips on it with their hose and say, "Well, it's coming through us." It's going to go to anybody who's hungry.

It's about to hit the Word of Faith churches. Restoration! Restoration! Restoration! Restoration! But you've got to be touched by that anointing . . . This is a different type of anointing — it's much stronger. It's different, but it's wonderful. It's strong. It penetrates. It's penetrating in the body of Christ, those who are hungry for it.

The anointing is going to touch and it's going to revive. It has to move out in our communities to do that. It's going to be similar to the revival that occurred through the ministry of Maria Woodworth-Etter . . . That anointing is going to raise dead people alive. It's going to be that anointing. In these last days, people got off in the ditch over it — the last day Elijah. It's going to be that kind of anointing in these last days . . . We're right on the verge of it, but the Church — it's going to happen in the Church. The anointing is breaking depression off the Church.

They're going to come through the doors stinkin', earrings all over their body. They're going to have tattoos from head to toe, but the anointing's going to hit them and they're going to cry out, "My God, I need to go to a place where they're going to give me the Word of God. I need help. Will you set me free with what you've got?"

This revival is going to break ranks and go over the denominational barriers. It's going to go over everything and it's going to start flooding, but it's got to start flooding in here first, in the local church. Pastors need to get before God as never before and say, "God, I'm hungry! I'm sick and tired of preaching canned sermons. I want to go into that pulpit with fire shooting out of my mouth!" And revival will break out. It'll start breaking out on the banks. It'll start moving out in our cities. . . .

The flood also brings judgment. People don't realize there's a two-edged sword there. It destroys the yoke and if you become a yoke to the body of Christ with your false doctrines and all your junk, you'll be removed. . . .

Get ready. Just sit in the boat. "Oooh, here comes another building. Here comes another jet, man. It's just so sweet being in this river, Lord. A few little ripples but that's all right, few persecutions. Hallelujah! Here comes the money! Here comes the building! Here comes the equipment! No toiling. No pulling."

"How goes the battle?"

"No, I'm not in a battle. I just get my prophecies out and let them fight for me. Believe the prophets and you shall prosper. I speak the Word and let it fight the good fight of faith. . . ."

I went back and looked at the people in the boat. God brought me back to the other boat and they were looking at their dry preacher and then they were looking over here seeing those people singing and shouting and they started jumping out of the boat and running over there and jumping in that other boat. The ones that are hungry will come to where the river is flowing in their churches.

This river's going to be a river of holiness. This anointing's stronger. Preachers, you're not going to be able to get away with stuff that we kinda got away with. We've got to be holy.

Fresh Oil Conference - May 6, 1997
World Harvest Church
Murrieta, California

I've never seen anything like that before, you might say, but that's this river. This river's full of joy. This river's full of deliverance and reviving and restoration. The anointings that many of you ministers operated in at one time are being restored right now. Restoration is in this river.

See, when a river's flowing, it starts to go over the banks. Now it's going over the banks. Things you wouldn't do in the natural you'll do in the supernatural, unfashionable things to religious folks, unfashionable things to the religious mind. This might be new to some of you, but it isn't new under the sun.

Fresh Oil Conference - May 7, 1997
World Harvest Church
Murrieta, California

Listen to the prophet. Listen to the Spirit of the Lord. God is raising up women in this day and in this hour. They have been suppressed and they have been put down because of gender, but I put My hand on whom I want, saith the Lord of hosts, and I'll raise them up as a sign and a wonder. And you'll see them rise up with the anointing and the power.

Did I not say, did I not say, did I not say, and My handmaidens, I'll pour it out on My handmaidens and they will prophesy and they will preach and they will teach under the fresh anointing in this day and this hour? And they'll jump in the river and they'll flow and they'll come up with the gifts that I have put into them and you'll see this surely come to pass in just days ahead.

Fresh Oil Conference - May 8, 1997
World Harvest Church
Murrieta, California

The Lord is saying to me that this anointing, this river that is flowing right now in the body of Christ is reviving and bringing restoration — restoration in the body of Christ. Neglected opportunities bring regret. There is so much opportunity right now to jump into what the Spirit of God is saying. To neglect that opportunity to jump in the river and make those changes to get into that river is really neglecting the opportunity that is flowing from heaven right now. The Holy Spirit is moving right now in a special way and now's the time to take those opportunities to say and believe. He's also bringing restoration to dreams that were put aside or delayed. Our ministries are being revived. There's some things that have been lost, and God is restoring anointings that were laid aside.

Every generation has the right to see the power of God. What we're stepping in right now — our foot is in it. As a matter of fact, the door is open and we got our foot in there. Those who are going with the stream — the foot's in there and the door's starting to open into that room that God wants us to come into.

There isn't a human being in this building who is alive today who has ever seen what you will see and what is about to happen in the area of miracles, signs, and wonders. You might have seen a little bit here and there, but what we're stepping into is the most phenomenal thing. At the turn of the century they had healing rooms — Dowie — miracles, signs, and wonders. Yeomans had healing rooms right here in Redondo Beach. John G. Lake had tremendous miracles — outstanding things happen. Maria Woodworth-Etter moved in the power of God — fifty miles that way, fifty miles this way — a hundred mile radius people would start falling out under the power of God.

What is happening right now is that the Church is being refreshed. The body of Christ is being refreshed with joy, and people are just fighting that. Then you've got those who are going in a ditch and they're making the First Church of Laughter. They're making the manifestation the end result, and that isn't what God wants. God has a job description for the anointing which is to destroy yokes and remove burdens. Always keep that in mind. That's the reason the anointing's coming and why it is here — to revive.

The fivefold ministry is going to operate so strong before we leave this planet earth. You're going to see pastors who we really, in this generation, haven't seen — with a strong backbone, strong anointings, strong leadership. He that followeth the sheep gets "doo-doo" on his feet. These men are not going to have any "doo-doo" on their feet. They're going to be strong leaders. They're going to point the sheep to righteousness and the sheep will grow up under this anointing of the shepherd that God is raising up today.

This generation doesn't know what a true evangelist is . . . The evangelist is going to come on the scene with miracles, signs, and wonders — outstanding things. And, what looseness we have used in connection with the apostle! People don't know much about that office. Little young guys saying that they're apostles and they have no idea what is involved in being an apostle. Dr. Lester Sumrall was an apostle. He walked with a tremendous amount of authority. Don't mess with the apostle . . . Teachers are going to flow with such a new anointing. Revelation is just going to flow out and people are going to go, "Oh, my goodness," and just "oooh" and "aaah" – not at the man, but at the revelation that is coming out in the teaching, and people are going to grow up from the Word of God. Shepherds . . . true shepherds are the ones who feed the sheep. And the buildings are not going to be able to hold the people. The anointing of God is going to be so strong. Believe His prophets and you shall prosper.

Tremendous things are happening. God is moving, and we need to be sensitive and move with Him. Neglected opportunities bring regret. You don't want to have regret . . . Spectators stand on the sidelines and don't jump in.

A woman as a sign and a wonder to the male generation — Aimee Semple McPherson — a woman who was really an apostle to her generation. When women couldn't even vote, she was in the ministry — had a strong anointing. Today in this hour, God is raising up strong – not arrogant, not unfeminine – women, women who are feminine, but through the power of God; and when they stand up in the pulpit, they do not have to bring attention that they are a woman. People will recognize right away — no gender — that there is an anointing on that woman. God is going to raise up women in a powerful way. This generation needs it. And you're going to see that.

This generation doesn't know much about trances, but we're going to get more into that. Why? Because it's a sign and a wonder and it reveals things . . . You may not need visions, but there's a world out there that needs visions. There's a world out there that needs signs and wonders. I don't need it to believe in God, but there's a dying world that has laughed at the Church and called us powerless and spineless, but that day is coming to an end because they're going to be scared of us — a reverent fear of the Church. "Don't mess with those folks."

Wait until you start seeing people stood up on their feet under the power of God as a sign and a wonder. This is what we're coming into. Wait till you see the rebellious come and they can't talk. It's going to happen . . . It's going to be done by the anointing of God. Then, this anointing, this joy is going to go out of the four walls. Wait till you see the whole church start quaking. The anointing also has a two-edged sword. It has another side of it. What people have been getting away with now, they won't get away with under the anointing of God in this revival.

There's going to be a revival of healing. You're going to

141

see healing rooms. You're going to see these miracles happen in a strong way. I had a vision this afternoon. I saw it. I saw it in the back room. I was starting to see it. I saw the healing rooms — people coming, wealthy people coming, wealthy people coming — flying in from all over because the word gets out. Wealthy people telling the other people, "Well, we've spent millions and could get no help. But, I know of a place. . . ."

Neglected opportunities bring regret. We're getting back into the Spirit. We're getting caught up in that river and in that river are signs and wonders and miracles and healings and deliverance for this world.

Here's an angel. An angel's come into this building. He's releasing a scroll and it says on the scroll, "Now is the time. Now is the time to step into it. Now is the time to step into healings. Now is the time to step into signs and wonders and miracles and walk in that river and walk in that flow. Now is the time. Now the time has come. Draw near. It's getting close to the end. It is close to the end. It is getting close to the end." There he goes. Glory!

The equipment has been given. The ability has been given. It is here. We have received the ability to do what God has called us to do. The Spirit of God is moving right now. We need not to neglect what God is doing this day and miss it because we are stuck in a rut. We need to come out of the rut and move with God. They're coming from every denomination and they're getting in the river — anybody who is thirsty. Anybody who is hungry can get into the river.

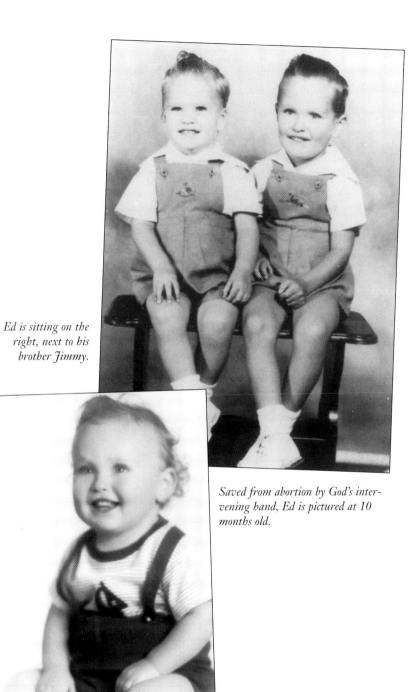

Ed is sitting on the right, next to his brother Jimmy.

Saved from abortion by God's intervening hand, Ed is pictured at 10 months old.

Ed is second from the left, with his 2 brothers and cousin.

Ed is pictured on the right with his brothers, Jimmy (left) and Danny (middle).

Ed's parents, Edward and Norma are seated with four of their five children. Ed is the one standing. Below Ed is Jimmy, Danny and Kathy (Patty isn't born yet).

A refreshing treat on a hot day shared by Ed's two brothers and cousin. Ed is second from the left.

Edward F. Dufresne, Sr., Ed's dad, shortly before his death in 1994 at the age of 71. He's now in heaven.

Ed as a teenager.

The best seat in the house! Stephen
is 11 and Grant is 2

Stephen & Grant Dufresne in 1999

Carole Dufresne-De La
Fuente, Ed's oldest Daughter

Suzie Dufresne Penir, Ed's
middle daughter

Stephanie Dufresne-Denton,
Ed's youngest daughter

Ed visiting the slums of the Phillipines while on tour with Dr. Sumrall. Below, Ed is passing out tracts.

Laying hands on a little girl while she holds tight to her doll.

Rejoicing with the people of God during the late 1970s

This is the note of encouragement Dr. Lester Sumrall left under the glass top on Ed's desk during a time of great testing.

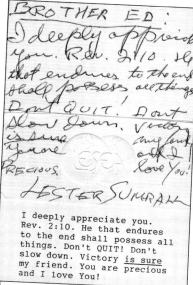

I deeply appreciate you.
Rev. 2:10. He that endures
to the end shall possess all
things. Don't QUIT! Don't
slow down. Victory <u>is sure</u>
my friend. You are precious
and I love You!

Dr. Lester Sumrall from whom Ed received many mighty impartations. He was Ed's mentor and pastor.

Dr. Lester Sumrall and Ed Dufresne on the set of Dr. Sumrall's daily television program.

Having just eloped, Ed and Nancy take off for a day and a half honeymoon in the plane given to Ed by Jerry Savelle. Then it was on the road again....

Ed and Nancy in 1987.

Ed and Nancy in 1995.

Ed is a little out numbered in the midst of all the females. Ed and Nancy with Ed's daughters. From left to right: Suzie, Carole, Ed, Nancy, Stephanie.

A little time of leisure.

Covenant brothers, Ed Dufresne & Kenneth Copeland. Kenneth Copeland was the man who first taught Ed about his covenant with God.

Ed preaching

Imparting God's healing power

Kenneth E. Hagin, Sr. is forever honored as Ed's spiritual father.

Mom and Dad Hagin with Ed and Nancy Dufresne at mom Hagin's 80th birthday party in 1998. No one could ever replace our spiritual Mom & Dad.

The Dufresne family. Ed and Nancy pictured with their two sons, Stephen (14 years old) and Grant (5 years old).

Ed is pictured in 1968 with his two oldest daughters, Carole and Suzie. He had only been saved a couple of years at the time.

Nancy's parents, Kenneth & Carolyn Chapman

Ed, receiving an honorary doctorate of Divinity from Bethel Christian College in June of 1991

3757798

UNION MISSION ARMY

INCORPORATED

THIS CERTIFIES THAT THE BEARER

ED. DUFRESNE

ORDAINED MINISTER OF THE GOSPEL
ACCREDITED AND QUALIFIED AS A
U. M. A. CHAPLAIN
AND A MEMBER IN GOOD STANDING

'77
ID UNTIL   GENERAL COMMANDER

Ed's first ordination card he received through the mail for $5.00

Ed preaching the uncompromised Word.

First church building in Torrence, CA.

Recording his Jesus the Healer radio broadcast, (early 1970s).

This is the building that was paid off after the angels appeared to Ed.

The building in Tulsa, nearing completion in 1987.

The Denver Hilton Hotel lobby where Ed received the healing anointing in his right hand.

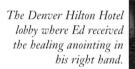

Teaching God's Word in the late 1970s

Ed Dufresne is committed to ministering God's healing power to the sick

Rejoicing in Jesus the Healer

Ministering God's Word on television in 1985

January 23, 1999
World Harvest Church
Murrieta, California

There's darkness in the world, but it's time for victory in the Church. Victory in the area of finances, victory in the area of healing, victory in the area of deliverance for the Church.

Don't let your heart be troubled. Don't let your heart be troubled, for these things have come to pass. But the gospel, but the gospel will be preached all over the world. It's been stored up. It's been stored up. It's been stored up. I'm talking about gold and silver. I'm talking about money. But it's ready to come over into the hands of those whose hearts are right concerning the wealth. I will not allow it to be transferred to those whom it would ruin and destroy. But those who have a giving heart, those who are tithers, those who are givers, they're the ones who will be funders in these last days.

It's time to laugh. It's not time to cry. It's time to laugh. Even this place, even this ministry, has stepped into a new day. And as you came into the new year, this place has changed. The place, you're in that spot. Oh, yes, many years the anointing has been held back. To a degree it had been released, but now it is unleashed, and now things will speed up. Things will speed up in this ministry, in the body of Christ. It'll speed up. It'll speed up, for the time is short. The end is near. But that time of My anointing, that time of My outflow of miracles, salvation, and harvest are in that time so be in position. Be in right position. Quit flopping around, saying, "I wonder if I'm in the will of God." Find out and get in it at any cost.

I hear this in my spirit — Get with it. Get with it. This is the time to get with it. This is not the time to be troubled. Get with it. Get out of your head and get into the spirit. God is depending on you getting into His will so He can fulfill what He has called you to do in your lives and in our lives, in this church, in the ministries He's called us to walk in.

New Albany, Indiana
July 15, 1999

What is that? What is that? What is that? I see an ocean. I see a wave. Oh, it's a wave, and the gifts are in this wave. There's a wave of the gifts of the Spirit about ready to hit America to those who are hungry. Oh, hallelujah! The working of miracles, the gifts of healings, the gift of faith in operation. In operation, IN OPERATION. And increase.

We've seen so much up to this time. A little dab here and a little dab there, but now it's going to be an ocean. An ocean of these gifts in operation. In OPERATION.

It's going to overtake us. It's going to overtake us like a tidal wave would come and overtake homes and overtake people. It's going to overtake us. And we'll look back, we'll look back and say, "Oh, God, it's so good, it's so good, it's so good, it's so good, it is so-ooooo good."

And then on the other side of the wave, there will be no more borders. In this wave there will be no more borders. There will be no measure in these gifts. It will be the full measure working in the body of Christ. All the revivals, all the way since

Jesus' time, all the moves of God, will all come in this wave. It will all be in one wave. All the power, the miracles, the demonstrations.

And disease, in this revival, will depart. Disease will depart. Even the medical industry will say, "This has to be God." The honest ones will have to say that.

So stir up the hunger. Stir up the hunger.

Blountsville, Alabama
July 25, 1999

Many changes — many, many changes coming to the body of Christ. Some good changes, but there's going to be those who will make the wrong decision and will go the other way and back off from the things of God. And it will get darker and darker for them.

But there will be those in the light of the Word of God who will not compromise. They will go forward and they will get stronger and stronger and – oh, my, the people who they will influence. Hallelujah! The people who they will influence for the kingdom of God will be great!

Jackson, Mississippi
August 15, 1999

Oh, I see that, Lord. I see that. I see that. When are these things going to come to pass? When are these things going to come to pass? Very shortly. Very shortly. I've been seeing it in my spirit. As I was sitting over there a few minutes ago, You were showing me again.

I keep seeing the ambulances. I see the crippled. We haven't seen this in the last . . . seems like, God, that You've just been quiet in the area of miracles. Oh, we've seen a little here, a little there, but not compared to the way it was during the healing revival; but it's going to happen again. It's going to happen again. It's going to happen again.

Stretchers coming out of the insane asylum, coming out of the hospital. Now, Lord, how can that be where there is so much trust in medical help today, Lord, more so than in You? Hallelujah, and what you're about to do. Oh, my, my, my, my. Praise God . . .

The more we get hungry for these things . . . We're coming into a revival of miracles, signs, and wonders. Only to those who will trust Him and only to those who will have faith in them, and only to those who will reverence and praise and worship Him.

Jackson, Mississippi
August 16, 1999

The days ahead are days filled with glory and days filled with power, so learn now how to flow and operate in a way that is pleasing to Me and in a way that will release it at its greatest measure because that power is needed to accomplish what it is that I want to do in this earth.

So use, use, use these days ahead to learn how to walk

with Me in a higher place. So take advantage of this time because there will be a time when the church will be running as never before to keep up with My glory. And in places and in cities and in nations where it was spoken that God will never get His way here, let it be known I will get My way there.

Jackson, Mississippi
August 17, 1999

You see, there is a heavier anointing coming to the Church. It's coming. It's right on the horizon of this planet earth so we must learn. We must be faithful. We must be faithful in our church. We must be faithful in our job that God has called us to do and be proven to walk and to carry this cloak of this type of anointing saith the Lord.

Part III
Classic Sermons

Sermon 1

Faith That Won't Give Up

What if a famous, macho movie star knocked on your door and demanded, "I want you out of this house in three minutes! Take all your clothes with you. I'm taking everything you've got — your wife, your children, and your bank account!" What would you do?

I'll tell you what *I'd* do. I'd say, "You and what army?"

That's what we're supposed to do when the devil knocks on our door and announces, "I've got some cancer for your family. I've got some poverty for your family."

Instead of replying, "Oh, come on in," it's time to be men. It's time we quit being wimps and stand up and say, "My Bible says this, and I will not be ashamed of the gospel!"

(You young girls who aren't married yet, don't marry a wimp. Marry a tongue-talking, healing-believing, devil-casting-out man who won't shut up about the gospel!)

Some of you go to church only on Sunday mornings, and you're backslidden and don't even know it. There are different ways to shut up. For example, most Full Gospel Christians are even afraid to pray out loud, such as saying grace in a restaurant.

Smith Wigglesworth wasn't afraid to pray in public. When he was ready to say grace in a restaurant, he'd ask all the other diners to be quiet, and then he'd pray. I'm not telling you to do that, but it's pretty bold. His friends report that everyone bowed their heads.

When the devil knocks at my door, I say, "Mr. Devil, you aren't having my wife. You aren't having my children. You aren't having my finances. And you aren't having my health! Get out of here, in the Name of Jesus! You have no right around here. I keep my premiums paid up!"

Bartimaeus Wouldn't Shut Up

And many charged him that he should hold his peace: but he cried the more a great deal, Thou son of David, have mercy on me.
Mark 10:48

Blind Bartimaeus wouldn't shut up. I don't like the word *The Living Bible* uses here, but it makes it real: *"'You lucky fellow,' they said, 'come on, he's calling you!'"* (v. 49).

That's amazing! One minute the crowd was telling him to shut up, and the next minute, after they saw that Jesus had stopped for him, they changed their attitude toward Bartimaeus.

Maybe people call you a "religious fanatic," but when they see healings taking place all around you, everyone you pray for gets healed and delivered, and God takes care of all your needs, they'll change their attitude about you.

Give Jesus first place in your life. Put Jesus first in your home. Put Jesus first in your office. Put Jesus first in your finances. Put Jesus first in every area of your life!

Jesus Stopped for Faith

Bartimaeus wouldn't shut up. The story continues:

> *And Jesus stood still, and commanded him to be called. . .*
>
> Mark 10:49

I like that. I'm not shutting up when it comes to the Word of God. If it's in the Word, I'm going to believe it. I don't care if it harelips the devil; I'm going to do what God told me to do. I will not shut up!

How would you like to be commanded by Jesus to come to Him? It reminds me of a game my little boy and I used to play. I would chase Stephen around the house until I got tired. Then I'd sit down, and he'd say, "Get me, Daddy! Get me!"

I say that all the time to God, "God, get me! Get me, get me, get me!"

"Thy Faith Hath Made Thee Whole"

> *And they called the blind man, saying unto him, Be of good comfort, rise; he calleth thee.*
>
> *And he, casting away his garment, rose, and came to Jesus.*
>
> *And Jesus answered and said unto him, What wilt thou that I should do unto thee? The blind man said unto him, Lord, that I might receive my sight.*
>
> *And Jesus said unto him, Go thy way; thy faith hath made thee whole. And immediately he received his sight, and followed Jesus in the way.*
>
> Mark 10:49-52

Notice, Jesus said that type of begging was *faith*. Do you understand what that kind of faith is?

First, blind Bartimaeus set a goal that he was going to get to Jesus. You must understand that he looked at Jesus in that

153

era differently from the way we do today. He looked at Jesus as a prophet of God, because he knew the mantle that was on Him.

So did the woman with the issue of blood. She said, *"If I may touch but his clothes, I shall be whole"* (Mark 5:28). Another translation says, *"If I may touch His mantle, I shall be whole."*

The Touch of Faith

In the Old Testament, people used to go to the prophet and make a demand on his mantle or anointing.

You remember the story in Second Kings 4 of the Shunammite woman whose child died? He was out in the fields with his father when he suffered a sunstroke. His father carried him into the house and placed him in his mother's lap.

She, in turn, lay the dead child on the bed in the chamber reserved for the prophet Elisha, who stayed at their home when he was in the vicinity. She said, "I'll be back," and she set off to seek the prophet of God.

The Bible says that when you receive a prophet in the name of a prophet, you will receive a prophet's reward (Matthew 10:41). God told me the reward this woman received sixteen years later – her child being raised from the dead — was because she took care of the prophet.

So the people in the Bible days looked at Jesus differently, because He was walking under the Old Covenant as a prophet. Although He was the Savior, too, they didn't understand that yet. However, they knew how to make a demand on a prophet. They knew that the prophet had a healing anointing or mantle.

Be like blind Bartimaeus, who locked in on Jesus, the prophet of God. *Lock in to the will of God for your life, and don't shut up or give up.* Don't let religious people keep you from worshipping God.

Keep Your Eyes on Jesus

I am listening to the Word; I am not listening to the news that comes and goes. Jesus is the same yesterday, today, and forever. If people turn their back on God because a spiritual leader backslides, it means they had their eyes on man and not on Jesus.

Men will fail you. Your pastor can only do so much, but Jesus passed His test. If you want an example to follow, follow after Jesus. Go back into the gospels and see how He handled everything. He used the Word of God. He's my example, not men.

"Well, I heard about this man. They say he did this and he did that."

That's just the devil trying to get you to shut up about your convictions and what you believe. Believe in Jesus. Depend on Jesus. Don't depend on me or anyone else to get your healing, because I don't have it. *He who is in me is the One who does the healing.*

It is extremely important that we all be in the right position. Let's get in our position. Let's find out the will of God. Let's quit drifting around, just sitting in church and "taking" all the time. Let's start "giving" of our finances, our time, and everything else. Let's find out what the will of God is for us and then don't shut up. Just stay in there.

"Brother Ed, I need healing."

Then start studying the Bible about healing, and find out what the will of God is for you concerning healing. You've got to build your own faith up, lock in on it, and don't give up until you get it. Stay right in there, confessing, "It is written."

My Household Shall Be Saved

My dad has gone home to be with the Lord. He had been an alcoholic all of his life, and he tried to die on me five different times. But every time he'd get ready to die, something would happen, and the doctors just didn't understand it.

They didn't know it, but it was because I have a covenant with my heavenly Father to believe on the Lord Jesus Christ and I shall be saved — *and my household.*

Every time my daddy got seriously ill, he'd say, "Now, don't phone little Eddie." That's what he called me. He hadn't realized that I became big Eddie. In his eyes, I was still little Eddie. He'd say, "Don't you phone him."

I'd be in a hotel room and the Spirit of God would tell me, "Your dad's in trouble. Give him a call."

When Dad would answer, he'd ask, "How did you find out?" Then he'd stop and answer it himself, "Oh, I know. That Holy Ghost told you. Will you let me die in peace?"

I'd say, "No, not until you give your heart to Jesus."

When I was preaching in San Bernardino, California a

few years ago, I saw my dad come in the back of the church and sit down. He had a big beard. I said, "That's my dad!"

I had phoned him and asked him to come, but he said, "Nope." When he says nope, that's it. But he came. He was raised a Catholic. Once a year he'd go to church long enough to put his dollar in the basket and light a candle.

But he sat in my meeting for three hours. He raised his hands like the others, and when I prayed for everyone in the building who wanted to be saved to raise their hands, he raised his hands and prayed with me. Glory! I just refused to give up on him.

The devil had been beating me over the head with the fact that my dad wasn't saved. "You're traveling all over the world, and your dad isn't even saved!"

I would say, "You lying devil! I've got a covenant with my heavenly Father to believe on the Lord. If I didn't believe in Him, I wouldn't be running all over the country, preaching. I'd get a 9:00 to 5:00 job, buy a camper and a boat, and have vacations and be like everyone else."

In Love with Jesus

But I'm in love with Jesus. I can't stop traveling. I've got a burning in my heart to preach. In fact, I'm doubling up on my meetings. It just burns in my spirit that time is so short, and what we do for Jesus is all that's going to count.

We're seeing one of the greatest revivals in history starting to take place, a little bit here and a little bit there. We're in it. It's going to be the greatest revival the world has ever seen!

We're going to see more healings and more working of miracles than the world has seen since the Day of Pentecost. As a matter of fact, God has told me that this wave is going to be a combination of all the waves since Pentecost. All the history of all the waves is going to be in this one wave. Our church buildings won't be big enough to hold the harvest of people who are going to be saved.

Hospitals Will Be Emptied

There was a man by the name of John Alexander Dowie who ministered in Chicago around the turn of the century. He was arrested more than a hundred times in just one year for "practicing medicine without a license."

The medical industry was so angry at him for praying for the sick, they put lawsuits on him. God said that's what is going to happen in this next wave, because the hospitals are going to be emptied of their patients after they are healed!

The medical profession is going to put lawsuits on us, because most of their industry is geared by money and greed anyway. Do you think they're trying to get a cure for AIDS because they truly love the homosexuals? No, they stand to make billions of dollars if they could get the treatment to cure the disease.

I predict we are going to see homosexuals come to our churches by the thousands, if not the millions, in this next wave, because the only way they are going to get healed is through divine healing. They are going to have to repent of that sin and get delivered, and God will heal them.

I also predict that there are going to be a lot more diseases doctors won't have a cure for, and the only way people will be healed of them is to come to the church and look to a healing Jesus. I tell people, "Why don't you take the gos-pill?"

Learn the Will of God

I'm not shutting up about this. Bartimaeus heard that Jesus was walking by, and he didn't care; he was going to get to that Man. He was going to get what he went after.

That's what the Holy Spirit is saying to churches today. Find out the will of God, lock in on it, and then don't shut up. It doesn't matter what anyone says.

"Well, I don't know. . . . I don't know if you should try that divine healing stuff. I don't know about that baptism in the Holy Spirit, and I don't know about trusting preachers."

If everyone in a church would pay his or her tithes every Sunday, the finances of that church would quadruple. The church would be able to reach out in television and other areas God has given them a vision for. They'd be able to build that new building God has put on their hearts to build.

A Dead Man's Reactions

The Bible says we are to give our body as a living sacrifice. What happens to a sacrifice? It's dead, so it doesn't care what anyone thinks about it. I tell my body that all the time.

It says, "You can't. You go too much. You're tired. You can't take that." I say, "Shut up, body. You're dead. Dead bodies don't gripe." Dead bodies don't gossip or get sick either.

But understand, I don't go beyond wisdom regarding the care of my body. We do have to take proper care of our bodies.

My goal is to get people saved, healed, set free, and turned on to Jesus.

Sermon 2

Healing: God's Calling Card

Do you know what God's "calling card" is? People being healed! A person's illness never drew anyone to God.

Romans 8:28 is often quoted: *"And we know that all things work together for good to them that love God. . . ."* This verse, however, is referring to prayer, not to all the bad things that happen to people.

Your spirit, the Holy Spirit, and all of God's armor listed in Ephesians 6 will work together for good when you're spending time in prayer, praying in tongues and believing God.

When I first started out in my ministry, a man who claimed he was a Bible scholar came to one of my meetings. Although he had already had five years of college, he still didn't have a job.

A man walked into that meeting on crutches but carried them out. He was completely healed. Scars were disappearing. Eyes were being opened. Legs were lengthened.

But the whole time I was praying for the people, this so-called Bible scholar was muttering, "You can't do that! You can't do that! That's not what my Bible school taught!"

I said, "I'm doing it."

I didn't even know how to preach at that time. I just brought my tape recorder, set it up, and we listened to tapes by Kenneth E. Hagin, Kenneth Copeland, and others. Afterwards we had a healing service, and I prayed for the sick. That's all I knew.

Then I started repeating a few things our "guest speakers" had said. I was turned on to the Word, and God started giving me some sermons. Finally I started preaching the Word of God myself. Praise God, the anointing is on His Word, and people were saved and healed.

God Receives Glory When We Exercise Our Authority

Now Peter and John went up together into the temple at the hour of prayer, being the ninth hour.

And a certain man lame from his mother's womb was carried, whom they laid daily at the gate of the temple which is called Beautiful, to ask alms of them that entered into the temple.

Acts 3:1,2

When passersby saw the lame man at the gate, did they all praise God because of his infirmity? No, the reason he was lying at the gate was because he was begging for alms. That was his only means of livelihood.

Who seeing Peter and John about to go into the temple asked an alms.

And Peter, fastening his eyes upon him with John, said, Look on us.

And he gave heed unto them, expecting to receive something of them.

Then Peter said, Silver and gold have I none; but such as I have give I thee: In the name of Jesus Christ of Nazareth rise up and walk.

And he took him by the right hand, and lifted him up: and immediately his feet and ankle bones received strength.

And he leaping up stood, and walked, and entered with them into the temple, walking, and leaping, and praising God.

Acts 3:3-8

God got all the glory for the lame man's healing, not for his sickness. *"And all the people saw him walking and praising God"* (v. 9).

He praised God and they praised God. They praised God for his healing, not for the fact that he was sick all those years so he could be humble.

The lame man was expecting to receive some money from Peter and John, but he received something far better than money: The power in the Name of Jesus is what Peter and John gave him. They knew the Healer was present to heal this man.

God's power will work the same through any born-again believer as it did through Peter and John at the Gate Beautiful. Jesus gave us His Name and the authority to use it in Mark 16:17,18:

> And these signs shall follow them that believe; In my name shall they cast out devils; they shall speak with new tongues;
> They shall take up serpents; and if they drink any deadly thing, it shall not hurt them; they shall lay hands on the sick, and they shall recover.

If you're a believer, these signs will follow you!

How Does God Teach His People?

God revealed this message to me one day when a horrible teaching was going around that God was the one who was making people sick in order to teach them things.

Don't get me wrong: You *can* learn things out of sickness, but why should a bit have to be put in your mouth so you can learn something? God's way of teaching you is through His Word.

What does the Bible say? Isaiah 53 describes prophetically what actually happened when Jesus was on the cross. It teaches that as Jesus became sin for us, and as all our sicknesses were put on Him, His appearance was marred beyond recognition.

Also, the chastisement (meaning punishment by pain) needful to obtain our peace was put on Jesus. He paid the price for our redemption.

Chapter 54 of Isaiah talks about the redeemed. Verse 13 says, *"And all thy children shall be taught of the Lord; and great shall be the peace of thy children."* Taught of the Lord!

Second Timothy 3:16,17 says, *"All scripture is given by inspiration of God, and is profitable for doctrine, for reproof, for correction, for instruction in righteousness: That the man of God may be perfect, thoroughly furnished unto all good works."*

The Word of God is good for teaching and correcting. If you want to get corrected, get into the epistles. They will clean you up.

Jesus Teaches About Prayer

In Matthew 7, Jesus gave this teaching:

Ask, and it shall be given you; seek, and ye shall find; knock, and it shall be opened unto you:

For every one that asketh receiveth; and he that seeketh findeth; and to him that knocketh it shall be opened.

Or what man is there of you, whom if his son ask bread, will he give him a stone?

Or if he ask a fish, will he give him a serpent?

If ye then, being evil, know how to give good gifts unto your children, how much more shall your Father which is in heaven give good things to them that ask him?

Matthew 7:7-11

What is Jesus doing here? He's trying to paint an image in your spirit. "Ask, and you shall receive," He says. "God is a good God!"

Jesus is teaching about prayer in the sixth and seventh chapters of Matthew. And right in the middle of this teaching, in Matthew 7:15 He says, *"Beware of false prophets, which come to you in sheep's clothing, but inwardly they are ravening wolves."*

I looked up "ravening wolves" in the Greek and found it means "spoiling lights." What does the word "light" mean? "The revelation of the Word of God." There are false prophets going around the earth today, spoiling, or twisting, the revelation of your heavenly Father.

In Matthew 7:7, Jesus is trying to give you a good image of your Father. He says that God won't give you a snake if you ask for a fish. And right in the middle of telling you that God is a good God, Jesus warns you to watch out for false prophets.

People who don't know any better are going around and twisting the revelation of the Father. That's why the body of Christ has been in such darkness all these years, Christians have had the wrong revelation of our Father in heaven.

God's Will Is Healing

Years ago there was a Bible student who gave me a bad time in a Bible study. He told the group, "I know someone who didn't get healed." (What about the ones who did?)

He went on to describe a beautiful young woman lying in a hospital room, dying with a disease. He painted such an appealing scene. He told about the nurses this girl won to the Lord before she died. He said that God had allowed the sickness so she could win those nurses.

"Isn't that wonderful?" he concluded. Some of the people began to weep.

I was preaching the Word of God to them, and here they were, crying over a poor girl who had died five years before, after winning some nurses to the Lord.

God could have healed her, and she could have won 500 people to the Lord and gone home to heaven at eighty years of age! After all, *there's a Healer in the house!*

Why do you have to be *sick* to go to the hospital to witness? Why don't you go there anyway?

If you're sick in a hospital, God will take advantage of the situation and show His love through you to the lost who are there. But that isn't His perfect will for you. He'd rather you win the whole hospital to the Lord *while you're well.*

If sickness is a blessing from God, then my mother was blessed tremendously. She was in and out of institutions most of her life. She was constantly sick.

People try to tell me that *God* did that. I'd rather serve the devil if that were true, but it isn't! It was Satan who did that to her, not my God.

Should You Praise God for Sickness?

You can praise God *in* sickness because the manifestation of your healing is coming — but you shouldn't praise God *for* sickness.

Do you know what god you're praising when you praise God for sickness? You're praising the god of sickness, who is Satan! You may not know it, but you are.

God is not the god of sickness. He doesn't have any sickness.

Doctrines saying that God wants some people to be sick come from the pit of hell to make the Christian double-minded. Jesus never turned anyone down who asked Him for healing. He didn't say, "You must keep your leprosy for a while." No, He said, "Your faith has made you whole!"

Jesus' attitude always was and is, *"What can I do for you? What can I do for you? What can I do for you?"* He never turns anyone down — but He never forces healing on anyone, either.

Jesus responds to faith, not to whims. He doesn't suddenly decide, "I like this fellow. He's good looking, and he's got a nice moustache. I think I'll heal him of that cold." The Lord doesn't have any favorites. Although He put me in a healing ministry, I have to believe Him for my healing, too.

I woke up one morning with a throbbing headache. It was still pounding after I got to the office. It would have been so easy to give in to it and go back home, telling myself, "I think I'll lie down. No one will miss me. I can read my Bible in bed. I need a rest anyway; I've been working too hard."

That's what the devil told me to do. I said, "You're a liar, devil! Healed men don't lie in bed when they should be working."

I remained at the office, stood on God's Word that says I'm healed, and received the manifestation of my healing.

There's a Healer in my house!

The Word: Anointed To Heal

Early in my ministry, a certain man told me, "You don't

167

pronounce words correctly. You'll have to go to speech school for ten years before you can preach." He almost had me convinced. I almost quit preaching the gospel.

Finally I realized that if I'm preaching the Word of God, I don't need to worry about how it comes out, because it's anointed. God will anoint the preaching of His Word.

Promote the Word, and the Word will promote you. I don't care where you are in life — promote the healing Word. If you need healing, promote the Word and you'll be promoted into health.

When the storms of life come your way, act like an eagle. Spread your wings of faith. The wind of the Holy Spirit will pick you up, and you'll soar over all those trials.

That's what an eagle does. When an eagle sees a storm coming, he locks his wings in a flight position. When that big storm comes — sickness, trials, tests — the winds lift him up above it. He can soar thousands of feet high, and he'll stay up there while the storm is blowing, raging, and tearing everything up down below. He just soars above it.

All the chickens down in the chicken coop will be running around looking for someplace to hide while Mr. Eagle soars safely up above the storm. When the storm is over, he comes back down.

Turned on to the Word

I thank God for His Word. After being saved for four years, I said, "Phooey on this religion junk!" I was filled with the Holy Spirit. I was a deacon and a greeter in the church. I did everything — I even cleaned the toilets — but I was still unhappy.

The outside of my Bible was worn out, but the inside was brand new. I was a real Bible-toter. I carried it everywhere. I thought that was the right thing to do. "Look, I'm a Christian!" I was proclaiming.

I never got *inside* my Bible until 1971 when I went to Denver, Colorado, and heard Kenneth Copeland preach about the covenant man David. There I heard for the first time that I could stand on God's Word, for it is true.

Don't you dare tell someone to stand on the Word for healing and then tell them it might not be God's will to heal everyone. There *is* a Healer in the house!

Sermon 3

The Righteousness of God

And all thy children shall be taught of the Lord; and great shall be the peace of thy children.
In righteousness shalt thou be established. . . .

Isaiah 54:13,14

Many Christians are defeated in life because they haven't established the fact that they are the righteousness of God.

The way the devil defeats Christians is by beating them over the head with sin-consciousness all the time. He says things like, "You aren't anything but a dirty old sinner, and you're this and you're that — and remember the mistakes you made? God isn't going to answer *your* prayers!"

Do you know what I do when the devil tells me that? I look at myself in the mirror and say, "You righteous person, straighten up in the Name of Jesus! I am righteous, not by *my* choice, but by *His* choice."

Most Christians don't have all their spiritual armor on. One piece of the Christian's armor is the breastplate of righteousness. The Bible says in First Corinthians 1:30 that we are righteous because of what *He* did:

But of him are ye in Christ Jesus, who of God is made unto us wisdom, and righteousness, and sanctification, and redemption.

171

Jesus' Righteousness

I was saved in a Full Gospel church. They would always say, "Your righteousness is as filthy rags." The Bible also says in James that a righteous man's prayers avail much, so if we were only righteous, we could get so much done. There's no doubt that our righteousness is as filthy rags, but I'm not referring to my righteousness; I'm referring to *Jesus'* righteousness and what He has provided for me.

Notice what it says in Isaiah 54:14: *"In righteousness shalt thou be established."* This is one of the most important things you need to establish in your Christian walk — that you are the righteousness of God.

Then, after you establish the fact that you are the righteousness of God, the passage continues:

> *Thou shalt be far from oppression; for thou shalt not fear: and from terror* [fear is torment]; *for it shall not come near thee.*
>
> Isaiah 54:14

I go to a lot of churches, and a lot of people in those churches are depressed and oppressed. As a matter of fact, when I have healing lines, I say, "I want everyone who is oppressed and depressed to come up for prayer." Usually anywhere from 50 to 75 percent of the members come to the front for prayer.

When Depression Strikes

Preachers are not excluded from any of these attacks. Sometimes I get tempted to be depressed, too. If oppression or depression tries to get hold of me, I go right back to the Word of God and I continue to study.

I get the E. W. Kenyon book on righteousness or some good tapes on righteousness and go back through the Scriptures and establish the fact in me that I am the righteousness of God; that I am in right standing because of the blood of Jesus Christ.

And I examine myself to see if I have any sin in my life. If so, I get rid of it, because, *"If we confess our sins, he is faithful and just to forgive us our sins, and to cleanse us from all unrighteousness"* (1 John 1:9).

You'll never fight the devil — you'll never fight sickness and disease, poverty, financial problems, or any of these things — until you establish the fact of who you are in Christ. You'll never stand up to the devil until you know who you are!

And listening to the preaching in some churches, you won't know who the bad guy is, God or the devil. The way they preach, you won't know which one is the enemy.

I know, because I got saved in a Full Gospel church. As a matter of fact, I got kicked out of it after I got a book called *Healing the Sick* by T. L. Osborn. It's dangerous to get a book like that, especially if you're hungry!

Look Out, Devil!

There's something about it when you find out who you are in Christ, and that the devil has lied to you all your life. Look out, devil! How many of you ever got fed up with his lies and said, "Enough is enough. Get out of here, devil!" — and ran him off?

This passage from Isaiah 54:14 says *you will be far from oppression.* And the 17th verse says:

No weapon [or no instrument of war] *that is formed against thee shall prosper; and every tongue that shall rise against thee in judgment thou shalt condemn. This is the heritage of the servants of the Lord, AND THEIR RIGHTEOUSNESS IS OF ME, saith the Lord.*

No weapon! Notice the subject here is righteousness.

I have a sermon that is titled, "Moses' Rod, Jesus." It came about because I was thinking about the Name of Jesus, and I was thinking about the power of attorney that we have.

Just imagine the richest man in town coming to you and giving you the power of attorney to sign his name to any check you wanted and to take care of his affairs while he is gone. That's what Jesus did for you and me!

I started thinking about that, and it just came up in my spirit, "So it was with Moses, when he used that rod. The rod was his authority when he went before Pharaoh and said, 'Let my people go.'" Then, when Pharaoh's magicians produced rods that turned into snakes, Moses placed his rod on the ground — and it ate up the devil's serpents!

Use Your Authority on Your Problem

The Lord told me, *"That authority that split the Red Sea is the same authority you have in the Name of Jesus Christ!"* I don't know what your problem is, but you can split it open with the Name of Jesus!

But first you've got to believe in that Name when you pray. And you can't believe it religiously, like a lot of people do. They pray religiously. To them, it's like using a "lucky" rabbit's foot. Furthermore, don't ask for what you want "for Jesus' sake." If it's for anyone's sake, it's for your sake. Jesus is doing fine. *He doesn't need any help.*

Five minutes after they pray, some people say, "O God, what are we going to do now?" They never believed what they prayed, and they didn't ask for their petition in Jesus' Name.

Jesus said, *"Whatsoever ye shall ask in my name, that will I do . . ."* (John 14:13). I like to preach on that text, too.

Something That Works

Now I'm going to teach you something the Lord has taught me through the years. It has always worked for me, in both rough times and good times. If you hear someone preach something, but it never works, what good is it?

I like things that *work.* I'd rather go to a John Wayne movie than listen to some preachers. Why? You know John Wayne is going to *win* every time, because he's the good guy! Listening to some preachers, you can't tell who's the good guy — God or the devil!

In Mark 10:46 we read:

And they came to Jericho: and as he went out of Jericho with his disciples and a great number of people, blind Bartimaeus . . . sat by the highway side begging.

I call this "faith begging." It is a different kind of begging from the kind where someone sits motionless, puts his hand out, and cries, "Alms, alms."

The Faith God Honors

Bartimaeus' begging is characterized by "importunity."

He's a man who went after something, and he didn't leave it alone until he got it. That's the kind of faith God honors. That's the kind of faith Jesus stopped for, and He asked, "What is it that I can do for you?"

And the blind beggar said, *"That I might receive my sight."*

Do you remember what Jesus said? *"Thy faith hath made thee whole."* It was not the begging or the yelling that got the blind man his sight, it was his faith.

Let's read on.

> *And when he heard that it was Jesus of Nazareth, he began to cry out, and say, Jesus, thou son of David, have mercy on me.*
> *And many charged him that he should hold his peace. . . .*
> Mark 10:47,48

And as we saw, *The Living Bible* says they told him to *"shut up"*!

There are different ways for the devil to tell you to shut up; to get you to back off from what you're believing for. He'll say, "Don't trust preachers anymore. Don't believe God for your healing. Just shut up. Don't get carried away with all that faith stuff."

> *And many charged him that he should hold his peace: but he cried the more a great deal, Thou Son of David, have mercy on me.*
> *And Jesus stood still, and commanded him to be called. . . .*
> Mark 10:48,49

I'd love it if Jesus commanded me, "Ed, come here. I want to talk to you." How would you like Jesus to call your name and command you to come to Him? Would you like that? *God always honors faith.*

Faith Speaks from a Coma

Years ago, when we started our first church, a woman began attending and got hold of the Word of God. She had been in a denominational Full Gospel church all her life.

As she and her husband were driving home after one of our services, the devil tried to kill her with a stroke. They rushed her to the hospital. She went into a coma. The doctors said, "We want to operate, we've got to dissolve her blood clot, but it doesn't look too good."

So they called me since I was their pastor. She was still in the emergency room. Her parents, who were raised in a Full Gospel denominational church, were falling apart. They were having a fit. Mind you, this whole family, generation after generation, had been raised in Full Gospel churches.

But this woman and her husband had been attending our church, and we had been teaching them faith. We had been teaching them that it is God's will for them to be healed.

When I walked into the emergency room, I said, "What's the problem?" Even though she was in a coma, the woman heard my voice, and replied, "Brother Ed, give me the Word. I need the Word!"

The doctors jumped back and said, "How can she talk when she's in a coma?"

A Carrier of the Word

And God said to me, "It's because your voice has delivered the Word to her so many months. You were the carrier of that Word to her spirit." She'd heard my voice all that time, listening to all my tapes.

I started quoting the Word of God to her. Right away her parents almost pushed me out of that room. They were rude and said, "You're an occultist. Get out of here." But her husband said, "No, *you* get out of here. He is my pastor."

When I say, "Don't shut up with your faith," I'm talking about using your faith. I asked a woman from the church to take tapes of the New Testament and Brother Hagin's healing scripture tape to the hospital and play them to the sick woman over and over again, night and day.

Full Gospel Unbelief

When the patient's father brought their Full Gospel pastor into that hospital room, they ran that woman off, threw the tape on the floor, and sat down and talked about politics.

Of course, when her husband came in the morning, he told the man, "I don't want you in this room at all!" That didn't make him very popular.

Don't forget: In the middle of a war, you're not trying to win a popularity contest. The devil will use your family and other loved ones to steal your miracle. That's true, and you know it. I'm going to prove it to you.

The woman recovered from her stroke and did not have to have an operation. God dissolved her blood clot. She was partially paralyzed in her leg and part of her arm for a few years after that. Then the doctors told her she could never have another child, but she did have another healthy child.

And I guarantee you, if she would have listened to those Full Gospel preachers, she would be dead today. Thank God for a husband who stood in the gap and didn't allow that to happen! I praise God for her healing.

Sermon 4

Faithfulness

Wherefore he saith, When he ascended up on high, he led captivity captive, and gave gifts unto men.

(Now that he ascended, what is it but that he also descended first into the lower parts of the earth?

He that descended is the same also that ascended up far above all heavens, that he might fill all things.)

Ephesians 4:8-10

Notice verse 8 says that the Lord gave *gifts* unto men. What are these gifts? Verses 11 and 12 tell us:

And he gave some, apostles; and some, prophets; and some, evangelists; and some, pastors and teachers;

For the perfecting of the saints, for the work of the ministry, for the edifying of the body of Christ.

Every minister of the gospel is a gift to the Church. When God first began to deal with me about preaching the gospel, I had such a bad image of myself that I certainly couldn't see myself as a gift to the Church.

I had to renew my mind to the Word of God and build into my spirit the reality that I was anointed of God to preach the gospel of Jesus Christ.

Before you can have any success as a pastor or teacher, you must know in your own heart that you are a gift to the body of Christ. If you don't believe it now, then keep building that truth into your spirit until all the doubt is driven out.

181

Just as the anointing of Elijah was transferred to Elisha, so was the fivefold mantle of ministry — apostle, prophet, evangelist, pastor, and teacher – dropped upon men when Jesus ascended to heaven.

If you are in one of the classes listed here in Ephesians 4:11, then the mantle was dropped on you. You are one of those gifts, and you are responsible for that gift to the body of Christ.

Many people today are not faithful to their calling.

> *According to the glorious gospel of the blessed God, which was committed to my trust.*
>
> *And I thank Christ Jesus our Lord, who hath enabled me, for that he counted me faithful, putting me into the ministry.*
>
> 1 Timothy 1:11,12

It's important to be faithful, no matter where you are or what you do.

When I first got saved, I loved the Lord so much that I wanted to do anything I could for Him, so He put me in charge of cleaning the toilets in my church. (Never ask to do something unless you intend to follow through!)

For over a year I was faithful in cleaning the toilets in that church. I thanked God that He counted me worthy to serve Him; and for being faithful in it, the Lord told me that He was going to bless whatever I set my hand to. And He did!

I got so blessed that I ended up with two trucks and fifteen employees in my new toilet cleaning business! As the Apostle Paul wrote to Timothy, I thank Christ Jesus, my Lord, Who has enabled me to clean the toilets, for He counted me *faithful*, putting me into the ministry.

I was also in charge of cleaning the carpets and shining

the pulpit. One night while working, I was thanking the Lord for my pastor, and God told me He had counted me faithful and was going to promote me to door greeter. So I was faithful as a door greeter!

You know, it makes an impression on people how they are met at the door. Even when people wouldn't offer their hand, I would just grab them and hug them and tell them I loved them.

When the Lord found me faithful as a door greeter, He promoted me to deacon. Then He said, "Son, I've counted you faithful in these three things. Now you are going to preach the gospel."

No matter what you are called to do — whether it's toilet detail, deacon, pastor, or floor sweeper — be faithful in it. One of the biggest problems in many churches is that the pastor doesn't have enough faithful workers.

The ministry of helps is just as important to God as the ministry of pastor. Praise God for the men who have been faithful in holding another man's coat!

In Exodus 17:8-13, Israel fought against Amalek. Because Moses couldn't get the job done alone, God provided faithful men to hold up his arms until the sun went down — and Israel prevailed over the enemy.

When a church has a group of faithful workers, it can fulfill its vision. The Lord did a pruning on my ministry and it seemed like half the church was going to leave; but when the purging was over, I was left with a faithful group of people.

> So the last shall be first, and the first last: for many be called, but few chosen.
>
> Matthew 20:16

God does not want you to push your ministry. Promote the Word and you will be promoted. But on the other hand, I am convinced that few are chosen because many who are called have a lack of faithfulness.

I would consider it a great honor for God to tell me to be faithful to a man of God and give him all the help he needs. One of the biggest enemies a pastor faces is discouragement. That's why God puts men into the ministry of helps and expects them to be faithful in upholding the pastor.

Proverbs 28:20 says, *"A faithful man shall abound with blessings. . . ."*

Years ago I was faithful when God told me to go from California to Oregon and preach to twelve people. For one year I pastored a group of people in Smith Valley, out where there was nothing but ranches.

We met in homes. The Indians would come down from the hills, and I would pastor those people every Sunday night. I was faithful to them.

There were times when I would say, "Lord, am I always going to be stuck with these people way out here in the boonies?"

It's so easy to start looking at the numbers. I had a problem with that. We say, "I don't have 20,000 people in my church, so I guess I'm not successful." If you're obeying what God told you to do, you're having success!

While I was preaching back then, it was so easy to get my eyes on other men's ministries. I was always watching other people to see how they would do things in their ministries;

then I would try to imitate them, thinking it would bring me the same success. Finally, God told me that if I kept doing that, it would destroy my ministry. I had to be faithful to what God told *me* to do. So I learned to relax and be faithful where I was.

You need to let God develop you and your ministry. If you keep your eyes on men, they'll fail you. But God knows how to do it. Remember, it will take some time for God to build character in you. Be faithful with the little things and watch God load it on you.

> *He that is faithful in that which is least is faithful also in much: and he that is unjust in the least is unjust also in much.*
>
> *If therefore ye have not been faithful in the unrighteous mammon, who will commit to your trust the true riches?*
>
> *And if ye have not been faithful in that which is another man's, who shall give you that which is your own?*
>
> Luke 16:10-12

Some men are driven with ambition to get to the top. Many people are just driven to outdo other people. We should want to help other ministers and rejoice with them when they get blessed. We have to get rid of this competitive attitude and just be faithful in doing what God has told us to do.

> *His lord said unto him, Well done, thou good and faithful servant: thou hast been faithful over a few things, I will make thee ruler over many things: enter thou into the joy of thy lord.*
>
> Matthew 25:21

This is what the Lord meant when He said those who are last shall be first. Though you are only in charge of the little things at the end of the line, God will exalt you much quicker than any man could.

If God counts you faithful in what He told you to do, I can

guarantee you that He will promote you. You may feel inadequate for your position; but if God put you there, then you can fulfill it. He will give you the tools and He will give you the speech.

After I experienced how it feels to be humiliated before people, I told God I would never preach again.

But the Lord said, "You must be more worried about what they think of you than what they think of My Word. Now get out there and put it out!"

So I did, and He has given me the tools and the speech to do it.

God has counted me faithful, just as He will count you faithful. All you have to do is make the quality decision to be faithful where He puts you and let Him promote you.

Nothing could be more rewarding than to hear Jesus say to you, "Well done, thou good and faithful servant."

Sermon 5

The Father Careth for You

Be ye not unequally yoked together with unbelievers: for what fellowship hath righteousness with unrighteousness? and what communion hath light with darkness?

And what concord hath Christ with Belial? or what part hath he that believeth with an infidel?

And what agreement hath the temple of God with idols? for ye are the temple of the living God; as God hath said, I will dwell in them, and walk in them; and I will be their God, and they shall be my people.

Wherefore come out from among them, and be ye separate, saith the Lord, and touch not the unclean thing; and I will receive you.

And will be a Father unto you, and ye shall be my sons and daughters, saith the Lord Almighty.

2 Corinthians 6:14-18

God wants to be a Father. He wants to take care of you and me. He wants to bless you beyond your wildest dreams. But if we carry worry around, hang around people who are unequally yoked, and let the world get on us, God can't "careth" for us and bless us. Whoever you run around with is what you will become like. You can't run around with the world, and let God be a Father to you. The Bible tells us to *"come out from among them, and be ye separate"* (2 Corinthians 6:17).

He is not a Father to everyone who calls Him Father. You have to live right according to Second Corinthians 6:14-18, so He can bless you and take care of you and give you the things He promises you in His Word. Even a natural father desires to give his children everything — imagine what our Heavenly Father desires to give us.

If you won't let Him take care of you, then you are the one who is going to have to take care of your own needs, because you are carrying it. *He does not want you to carry cares!* His yoke is easy and His burden is light. Even when I don't feel like it, I laugh at the devil and stay drunk in the Holy Ghost.

First Peter 5:6,7 says, *"Humble yourselves therefore under the mighty hand of God, that he may exalt you in due time: Casting all your care upon him; for he careth for you."*

I want the will of God exalted in my life. Don't you? Then you have to find out what being humble means. A humble man is a man who will talk the Word of God in spite of the circumstances. You must speak the Word of God over your circumstances and use the prophecies that have been spoken over you to fight a good warfare. The Word of God never fails, and it is impossible for you to fail as long as you do what He tells you to do and walk in love.

God wants to take care of His people, but some won't let Him. Any good father wants to take care of his children. He loves you, and He cares for you, but if you are carrying discouragement, worry, and care around, He can't carry them for you. Worry is like saying, "I don't need You. I'll care for myself."

If we're not careful, even ministers can pick up the care of the ministry. I've done it myself.

Money isn't the problem. It's a spiritual problem. God meets all our needs according to His riches in glory. Money will not solve your problems. You have to get your tithing straight and your living right. Repent and roll all your cares over on Him. He wants to be your Father. He wants to care for you and bless you. Remember, He can't take the care if you are carrying it around.

There are two areas where people have a problem — money and authority. They don't want to grow up and be submitted to authority. They are babies and want to have things their own way.

God is raising up an army, but we have churches that are full of babies and fugitives. We need churches that are going to cause people to grow up. Ministers have to preach it and tell it like it is, and learn to cast the care of it upon the Lord. Never let people pull you down to their level. Pacifiers don't last long in boot camp. Remember that whatever you use to get the people to the church, you'll have to use to keep them. Use the Word of God. You don't want a nursery, you want an army.

The cares of this world try to get on all of us, but stay drunk in the Holy Ghost, and pray in tongues, building yourself up on your most holy faith, and those cares cannot get on you. *Confess and talk about the mercies and the goodness of God!* His mercies are new every morning. That means that even before you get up, mercies are there waiting for you when you open your eyes. We need to talk about the mercies of God. We need to talk about how good He is. We need to talk about how much He loves us.

God told me that His people worship Him, but they need to talk more about His tender mercies and how much He loves them!

You've got God on the inside of you. You've got God alongside of you. You're blessed! *"I will be their God, and they shall be my people"* (2 Corinthians 6:16). The Father left us an inheritance. He loves us! He said He would meet all our needs — spirit, soul, and body.

There are reasons why people fail — they worry. They get discouraged and begin to speak the problem. Discouragement is like a rattlesnake. You have to keep that thing out, or it will destroy you. Don't touch it with your thought life. We are to walk in faith and love. The devil will tell you all sorts of things about your children and how you're not going to make it, but what counts is what God says. Say that!

In Psalm 37:4,5 God tells us, *"Delight thyself also in the Lord; and he shall give thee the desires of thine heart. Commit thy way unto the Lord; trust also in him; and he shall bring it to pass."* You need to trust Him, that what His Word says is true. He will meet your needs! He will care for you! He will give you the desires of your heart! But you must delight yourself in Him. In verse 1 of Psalm, chapter 37, He says, *"Fret not...."* Do not worry. It is sin!

Philippians 4:4,6 says:

> *Rejoice in the Lord alway: and again I say, Rejoice . . . Be careful for nothing* [don't take the care]*; but in every thing by prayer and supplication with thanksgiving let your requests be made known unto God.*

We miss it on the thanksgiving part. He's talking about not carrying the care, but take care of it in your prayer life. You have to thank God by faith that He is taking care of it.

Everybody goes through things, even preachers. But you can't take things personally. In verse 5 of Psalm, chapter 37,

God tells us, *"Commit thy way unto the Lord. . . ."* That means to simply roll all your cares over on Him for He careth for you. There is a faith in knowing that He is going to take care of you. Wait patiently for Him. Rest in Him. Say, "It's not my care." When we walk in God's rest, we walk in victory.

God is your loving Father and He wants to take care of you!

Sermon 6

Faithfulness and Loyalty

Most men will proclaim every one his own goodness: but a faithful man who can find?

Proverbs 20:6

A faithful man is hard to find. It takes time to find out if someone is faithful, and it also takes time before someone has a chance to prove themselves faithful. You can't just take their word for it. Their actions must be observed and this takes time.

Many people are willing to help, but they never finish what they started, or they don't complete the task as ordered. Willingness is not faithfulness! Faithfulness is a characteristic of God Himself. You will find in Galatians 5:22 that faithfulness is listed as a fruit of the Spirit. (In the *King James Translation* "faith" is listed as a fruit of the Spirit, but in the Greek it actually says, "faithfulness.") So to be formed fully into the image of Christ, we must be found with the spiritual characteristic of faithfulness.

Faithfulness in Relationships

Faithfulness must begin at home. If you are not faithful to love, serve, protect, and honor your own spouse and children, it is impossible to have faithfulness toward another person outside of the home. If you're not willing to defend and speak well of your spouse to others, you're not faithful and will not be faithful to anyone else.

You must also be faithful at work to your employer. If you don't fulfill your tasks and assignments exactly as they ask without arguing, or you try to do things your own way when they're not looking, you're not being faithful.

When I was a teenager, I worked for a man named Mr. Goodwin. One day I overheard and agreed with negative conversation about Mr. Goodwin and was subsequently fired. Later, however, I repented and was rehired and given a raise. If you talk or think negatively about your employer in the smallest way, even though you may be right, or you just agree with other negative speaking employees, you're not faithful. You have no right to receive any kind of salary from an employer that you think ill of or speak ill about. If your employer can't depend on you at all times to do what he asked you to do, you're not faithful.

If you're not growing personally with your organization, employer, or church, you're not being faithful, and you will very likely end up having to leave. Personal growth is all a part of faithfulness and is a key to being used by God.

In First Chronicles 11:10 it says, *"These also are the chief of the mighty men whom David had, WHO STRENGTHENED THEMSELVES WITH HIM in his kingdom, and with all Israel, to make him king...."* These men strengthened themselves so they could further David's kingdom, not their own kingdom. They caused personal growth, not to establish themselves, but to establish David as king. Faithful men! A faithful man never has a hidden motive when serving and supporting another man's vision.

> *And if ye have not been faithful in that which is another man's,*
> *who shall give you that which is your own?*
>
> Luke 16:12

Serving in your church in any area of ministry is an honor, because it's God's work. As David said, *"For a day in thy courts is better than a thousand. I had rather be a doorkeeper in the house of my God, than to dwell in the tents of wickedness"* (Psalm 84:10). If you're not faithful, you can't even keep God's door!

Faithfulness is a basic quality you must possess just to become a candidate for serving in any area of ministry, but it's not the highest destination. Faithfulness is a necessary quality that you must develop just to be at the entry level into God's blessings.

> *A faithful man shall abound with blessings. . . .*
>
> Proverbs 28:20

Loyalty

Loyalty is above and beyond faithfulness. *You must be faithful to all, but you can only be loyal to a few.* You must be faithful to the entire body of Christ, but you can only be loyal to a few. If you're not careful, your faithfulness can become mechanical and mental in its actions; it knows the right thing to do. But loyalty is of the heart. God is loyal!

In the book of Samuel we read about Saul who knew that he had lost his kingdom spiritually. Consequently, he was jealous of David, the man of God who had been anointed to be king in his place. When someone has failed to fulfill their office, they are always jealous of the person God has chosen as a replacement.

This was not the case with Jonathan, Saul's son. Jonathan was next in line to become king, but he stripped himself of his kingly robe and honor, giving it to David, the man God had anointed to be king. Jonathan even protected David from his own father. A loyal person will always protect the anointing, the anointed one, and the will of God first. They will always protect these things.

The story of Jonathan and David is a classic illustration of true loyalty. Jonathan and David knew about faithfulness and loyalty. They took risks to protect the one they were loyal to, without any hidden motives or agendas.

First Samuel 18:1 says, *"The soul of Jonathan was knit with the soul of David, and Jonathan loved him as his own soul."*

Jonathan went against his own family to take sides with the anointed man of God. You must always be more loyal to God than you are to your own family members. In other words, put God and His will above the will of those closest to you. Obeying a family member, instead of God, will cost you the anointing.

Many people are only loyal to themselves and not to anyone else. The mark of a loyal person is that they will always cater to the likes of the leader, never to their own or to any else's. They serve out of their heart and don't need a reason to serve. Their loyalty is a product of their integrity.

God is a God of integrity, true to His Word, and always deals honorably with all men and in all situations. He demands no less from us. If you will work on your integrity, you won't have any trouble believing God, and God will prove you faithful in the ministry to which He has called you.

A faithful man is a joy to have around, but a loyal man is a gift from God!

Sermon 7

The Fatness of the Anointing

*And it shall come to pass in that day, that his burden shall be
taken away from off thy shoulder, and his yoke from off thy neck, and
the yoke shall be destroyed because of the anointing.*

Isaiah 10:27

The anointing of God destroys the yoke of bondage that
the devil has bound people up with. There is no way to
destroy Satan's work without the anointing. Jesus had to wait
to begin His earthly ministry until He was anointed by the Spirit
of God. Although He was the Son of God, He was unable to
accomplish God's work without the anointing and was unable
to destroy the devil's work without the anointing. If Jesus was
so reliant upon the anointing for His ministry, how true that is
with us. We are powerless without the anointing which the
Spirit of God manifests. The anointing works great deliverance
toward those who receive it.

The Amplified Bible brings out another dimension of the
anointing: *"And it shall be in that day that the burden of [the
Assyrian] shall depart from your shoulders, and the yoke from your
neck. The yoke shall be destroyed because of fatness [which prevents
it from going around your neck]"* (Isaiah 10:27).

Look at that word "fatness." That means "the fatness of
the anointing." Not only does the anointing destroy the yoke,

but when we are *fat* with the anointing, it prevents any yokes from getting on us. Talk about preventative medicine!

The way to stay free from yokes is to stay fat with the anointing!

Jesus got up and preached in His own hometown, saying:

> The Spirit of the Lord is upon me, because he hath anointed me to preach the gospel to the poor; he hath sent me to heal the brokenhearted, to preach deliverance to the captives, and recovering of sight to the blind, to set at liberty them that are bruised, to preach the acceptable year of the Lord.
>
> Luke 4:18,19

But right after He preached this great truth, all those who heard Him took Him to the brow of the hill and tried to push Him off the cliff, but the Bible tells us that He just walked off right through the midst of them. How did He do that? He was *fat* with the anointing and no yoke could get on Him.

When you face any test and trial, you can be assured that you will walk through it in total victory, when you are *fat* with the anointing. You can tell who is full of the anointing — those who walk in victory!

There is no reason for a believer to walk around all down and depressed. Just get in the anointing and fatten yourself up!

Jesus said that if you needed rest, just come to Him. Take His yoke upon you. His yoke is easy and His burden is light.

What is His yoke? It's the anointing.

In other words, His invitation to us is "get yoked up with the anointing." The devil can't yoke you up with his goods when Jesus has yoked you up with that anointing.

Jesus said that His yoke is easy. If life is hard for you, you're not yoked up with the anointing. The anointing makes life easy. The Bible says that the way of the transgressor is hard. If things are hard for you, somewhere along the way you have transgressed from God's plan for your life.

Get back into God's plan and you'll get back in the anointing and life will be easy for you once again.

People get burned out and knocked out of their spiritual race when they are trying to operate without the oil of the anointing.

A car's engine will burn up when it runs without any oil. Oil keeps the equipment operating smoothly. It's the same with the believer's life. The anointing keeps you oiled down and the enemy's yoke slips right off of you.

Get the anointing on all areas of your life and walk in the victory God intended for you.

Sermon 8

"I Ordained Thee a Prophet"

Any study of the office of prophet must include an examination of how a prophet is called.

The most important thing to consider is this: It is imperative that you know beyond any doubt that you are called of God to be a prophet. Your call must be confirmed until absolutely no doubt remains in your mind because, as James says, *"A double minded man is unstable in all his ways"* (James 1:8).

If I were on an operating table and a qualified doctor came in, saying, "Well, I don't know if I can do this or not," I'd yell, "Get this guy out of here!" The doctor had better have confidence in what he's doing before he operates on *me!*

Regardless of the call on your life, it's essential that you have complete assurance about your ministry.

You can know if you have a divine call by *conviction,* or by a *witness* in your spirit, and by a divine *compulsion* on the inside of you concerning the call that's upon your life. You can even know if you're called to be a prophet or not. It's the same way you can tell if you're a pastor or not; *the characteristics of that mantle will be on you!*

Prophecy Confirms, Never Calls

Here are some additional warnings and guidelines you can use to tell if you're really called into the ministry:

If someone prophesies that you are called to the fivefold ministry, but God hasn't told you, disregard the prophecy!

Sometimes I'll enter a church and a young man will get me in a corner, or slip into the pastor's office and whisper, "I'm a prophet."

I always reply, "Oh yeah? How do you know?"

He'll say, "Well, a guy here prophesied, or someone came through and prophesied over me that I'm a prophet. Uh, what do you *do* as a prophet?"

"Well, I *work*. I work in the gospel. I don't sit up on a mountaintop and prophesy all the time."

"Huh?"

The true New Testament gift of prophecy only *confirms;* it never *calls*. When people started prophesying over me about the different callings on my life, I already knew about them. The whole picture was still fuzzy to me, but their words confirmed what God was already dealing with me about.

Need vs. Call

Know something else: *A need is not a call*. Some people see a need, so they try to call themselves into the ministry in order to fulfill that need. In other words, just because they are *burdened* for Mexican orphans doesn't mean they are *called* to be a missionary to Mexico.

If you enter the ministry and God didn't call you, you will fail. But if you have that divine call, know it, and remain faithful to it, you will succeed.

I've known young men who have wanted to get involved

in the ministry. They've said, "God told me to do this for you. God told me to do that for you." But after a while, when the going got tough, off they went. They weren't called.

The Fight for Your Ministry

The devil will fight you for that call of God that's on your life. He will try to talk you out of it.

He doesn't want you in the position that God put you in.

Furthermore, the ministry is not easy — I don't care what anyone tells you. Believe me, there will be rough times, but you must remain faithful to your call during those times. You see, there's a price you pay to walk in the anointing!

You may be called upon to make great sacrifices, but the call alone will pull you through if you remain faithful. That's one way you can tell if you've got the call; just remain faithful to it, and that call will pull you through.

I had a rough time getting into the ministry. Every time I look back on my life, even on the tragedies, I say, "But I made it!"

If you think you are called to stand in a particular office, wait and test your call to find out for sure. Even if you are called to one of the ministry gifts, you won't step into it immediately; you'll start at the bottom.

If God exposed you to the full power of the office while you're still in training, it could destroy you and your ministry. You haven't learned how to be faithful yet. You haven't learned how to be consecrated yet.

Can you imagine a little baby playing in his crib with an

H-bomb? What if his daddy gave it to him and said, "Now, just push that button, and you'll have all the power you want." It's the same with the fivefold ministries; there's a lot of power in them, and it takes time — years, in fact — to learn how to operate them.

The Years of Preparation

When I was just starting out in the ministry, I was in a morning teaching service, and the power of God fell. I told a young man what God was showing me about him. Later, I felt I had grieved the Spirit of God.

I asked, "What is it, Lord?"

He said, "You shouldn't have told him. I revealed it to you, but you weren't to tell it now. You could hurt him, because he's so enthusiastic. But he'll be all right. You pray for him."

That's how I learned that there's a time to reveal things by the Spirit, and there's a time not to say those things.

Brother Hagin was in the ministry for eighteen years before he entered into the prophet's ministry. That office didn't come on him until he had spent many years in preparation for it.

If you are called to the fivefold ministry, use your years of preparation to study. Preparation time is never lost time.

Whatever your call is, you *must* build your ministry on the Word of God. You cannot build a ministry on the supernatural, or on a gift. If you will build your ministry on the Word of God, it will last forever because the Word is forever.

In the future, if sickness and disease come knocking on

your door, and if the gifts of the Spirit are not in operation for some reason, you're going to have to stand on the Word. And what if there's no prophet in town?

So dedicate, consecrate, and submit yourself to God's will in your life. Know that if God *calls* you, He will *equip* you to carry out that call. Your gift *will* make a way for you. Also, get involved in a local church. Do whatever your hand finds to do in the ministry of helps.

Dusting the Pulpit

I'll never forget the night I was dusting the pulpit, and all of a sudden a voice boomed out of the pulpit, saying, "You'll go all over the world and preach." I jumped! No one was around.

I thought my pastor was playing a practical joke on me, so I walked over to the loudspeakers and inspected them. But it was God speaking to me.

I replied, "God, I can't even get up and give a testimony, let alone preach! That ain't my calling. I'm a helper. I work with my hands. I can build buildings, and I can clean toilets. But I can't preach."

Even my pastor told me, "Ed, you'd have to go to speech classes for ten years before you could preach." If I'd have listened to him, I wouldn't be in the ministry today. But here I am, mistakes and all. I was faithful where I was, and a faithful man shall abound in the blessings of God.

As you remain faithful wherever you're at, God will bring you to the top, too. It happens every time. Cream always rises!

Called from My Mother's Womb

Yes, there are times when my knees shake when I get up to preach. However, I *know* what God has called me to do.

The Bible tells us in Isaiah and Jeremiah that a prophet is called from his mother's womb. One day the Lord gave me a vision of my whole life and revealed to me that I, too, was called from the womb. He explained my whole life up to that point in time.

For years, I hadn't realized that the prophet's mantle was upon me. This knowledge gradually unfolded to me. Things started happening, and God dealt with me about the anointing on my life.

However, I didn't understand much about it, because there was a lack of teaching on the office of prophet in those days.

Different men of God would come to town, call me out of the congregation, and prophesy about my ministry, but I was still in the ministry of helps then. I had the ministry of toilets.

That's right — for five years I cleaned the church toilets. Not too many ministers want to start out by cleaning toilets, but God's got to find out if you're faithful. *If you can't clean toilets for God, how are you going to prophesy for Him?* I hope you don't have to do that, but I was in bad shape.

When the Lord started dealing with me about ministry, I reminded Him, "Lord, I'm not an eloquent speaker." I could never get up and give a talk in grammar school, junior high, or high school (which I didn't finish). There were too many problems at home. My home was full of alcoholism, and I couldn't study under those circumstances, so I dropped out of school.

Several years ago, when the Lord gave me that vision of my life, He said, "Ed Dufresne, I know you. I ordained you and I sanctified you in your mother's womb to be a minister of the gospel."

Angels Halted My Abortion

In the vision, He showed me that my parents had decided to abort me a few weeks after I had been conceived! That was in 1940. My mother was fifteen, and my dad was just sixteen. That's pretty young. And World War II was about to break out.

My dad was an apprentice sheet metal man, and he couldn't afford to get married. So they talked about aborting me, and my mother was ready to go for the abortion.

And I saw what happened. I saw angels come down from heaven and stop it, because God commanded that I was ordained of God. The angels turned the situation around and my parents got married instead of having the abortion.

I was born in June 1941. I'm here. But if they had aborted me, I'd still be a human being, and I'd be in heaven now.

Let's take a little side trip here. When you get to heaven, you're going to see all the aborted children. They're there. Once, when God was dealing with me about an unwed mothers' home, I had a vision and saw these aborted children in heaven.

I also saw the women who had aborted their children. They thought they had gotten rid of them. Some of them, of course, later repent, and they can be set free of their sin and guilt.

I saw as the saved women walked through the gates of

heaven, and their aborted children greeted them, saying, "Mommy, I love you!"

That's the mercy and love of God! You know, parents can misuse or beat a child, and he'll still stick up for his parents. A judge may ask him, "Did your mommy and daddy do that?"

"No, my mommy and daddy didn't do it." That's why we ought to be like a child, they're very forgiving. Of such is the kingdom of heaven, Jesus said.

Until the Lord showed me this vision, I had never known that my parents had considered aborting me. Later, I asked my dad about it. He said, "Yes, sorry to say, that's true. We were going to abort you."

The Devil's Plot Against Prophets

The Lord revealed many other things to me. He went all the way through my life and showed me everything, explaining why things had happened and why people had behaved as they had.

I had many relatives on both sides of the family who were in mental institutions. When my grandfather found out my mother was pregnant with me, he committed suicide. He left a note to my mother, telling her that she was the reason he committed suicide — he couldn't handle her pregnancy. He felt degraded by her actions.

Then, of course, my mother had to live with that guilt the rest of her life, and that's what drove her into mental institutions.

My parents vowed they weren't going to become alcoholics. But after my brother was born, they started sipping little cocktails and having a little wine, and they did end up as alcoholics.

All of these things were geared to destroy that anointing that came out of my mother's womb – her son who was ordained a prophet.

Know this; the devil hates anointed men and women of God. He hates Christians, period, and he seems to particularly want to destroy prophets!

Look at Brother Hagin's life. He was born prematurely. He didn't even look like a human baby. The doctor and his Grandmother Drake couldn't detect any signs of life, so his grandmother put him in a shoe box and was going to bury him in the backyard!

But God's angels intervened to protect the prophet's anointing and his grandmother suddenly detected a little movement in the tiny body. He's still alive today, eighty some years later!

I appreciated God so much for taking me all the way back through my life and explaining everything that has happened to me. I learned that all the bad things were engineered by the devil to destroy the anointing that has been on my life from my mother's womb.

The devil is working overtime to destroy the anointing on the lives of *all* of God's servants. That's why we shouldn't get angry at the person who has fallen to Satan's wiles. We have no right to criticize such a person. We don't know all the stress and strain he has been under. We should just keep quiet and pray for him.

God's Call to Isaiah and Jeremiah

The Lord gave much the same commission to the prophet Isaiah that He did to Jeremiah:

> *Listen, O isles, unto me; and hearken, ye people, from far; The Lord hath called me from the womb; from the bowels of my mother hath he made mention of my name.*
>
> *And he hath made my mouth like a sharp sword; in the shadow of his hand hath he hid me, and made me a polished shaft; in his quiver hath he hid me;*
>
> *And said unto me, Thou art my servant, O Israel, in whom I will be glorified.*
>
> Isaiah 49:1-3

The following passage from Jeremiah reveals how God looks at His prophets. This is the assurance He gave the prophet Jeremiah:

> *Before I formed thee in the belly I knew thee; and before thou camest forth out of the womb I sanctified thee, and I ordained thee a prophet unto the nations.*
>
> *Then said I, Ah, Lord God! Behold, I cannot speak: for I am a child.*
>
> *But the Lord said unto me, Say not, I am a child: for thou shalt go to all that I shall send thee, and whatsoever I command thee thou shalt speak.*
>
> *Be not afraid of their faces: for I am with thee to deliver thee, saith the Lord.*
>
> *Then the Lord put forth his hand, and touched my mouth. And the Lord said unto me, Behold, I have put my words in thy mouth.*
>
> *See, I have this day set thee over the nations and over the kingdoms, to root out, and to pull down, and to destroy, and to throw down, to build, and to plant.*
>
> Jeremiah 1:5-10

Let's begin with the fifth verse: "*Before I formed thee* in *the belly I knew thee; and before thou camest forth out of the womb I sanctified thee. . . .*"

212

Isn't it amazing that people will abort children? Their excuse is, "Well, that was nothing but a *blob.*" But here God says, "I knew them before they were even formed. In the belly I knew them." *You don't know a blob!*

"*And before thou camest forth out of the womb I sanctified thee. . .*" This means that God set the prophet apart. "*And I ordained thee a prophet unto the nations.*"

And God Hath Set Some in the Church

First of all, God is the One who calls someone to the ministry. *God* does this – not dad, mom, family, or a church board. You can't set yourself apart as a prophet or any other gift ministry. You've got to be commissioned or ordained by God.

I believe in the fivefold ministries that Scripture tells us *God sets* in the Church of the Lord Jesus Christ:

AND GOD HATH SET SOME IN THE CHURCH, first apostles, secondarily prophets, thirdly teachers, after that miracles, then gifts of healings, helps, governments, diversities of tongues.
I Corinthians 12:28

AND HE GAVE SOME, apostles; and some, prophets; and some, evangelists; and some, pastors and teachers;
For the perfecting of the saints, for the work of the ministry, for the edifying of the body of Christ.
Ephesians 4:11,12

One day I was reading First Corinthians 1:28 and I asked the Lord, "What do You mean by 'set'?" My mind immediately went back to the years I was in construction work. I know what happens when concrete sets up.

When we poured concrete and it was still wet, we could

move it around, but once it was *set,* we couldn't move it unless we used dynamite. This is God's plan for the Church; He sets ministries in place.

It amazes me that people think they can call themselves into the ministry! I saw a TV preacher who said, "Bless God, if we need a prophet in our church, God will anoint *me* to be the prophet, and if we need an apostle, He'll anoint *me* to be the apostle."

I thought, *How ignorant can you get? That isn't what the Bible says.* The Bible says, *"And God hath set some in the church. . . ."*

Men cannot set the fivefold ministries in the body of Christ.

Sermon 9

The Double Portion

Do you know the story of Elisha and Elijah? Elisha was at the right place at the right time when Elijah's mantle fell.

The mantle doesn't *automatically* fall on a man of God just because his dad's a prophet. If the son is goofing off, doing his own thing, the mantle won't fall on him when his dad goes home to be with the Lord.

I believe you have to be in the right position with God, and you have to *want* that anointing more than anything in the world. Elisha wanted it that much, because he refused to leave Elijah.

When I was a young Christian, I couldn't figure this out. Then I started getting revelation knowledge about the relationship of Elijah and Elisha. I came to realize that you can receive a mantle through *association*.

I once worked alongside a pastor for five years, doing everything I could find to do — from janitor work to construction — in the ministry of helps. I didn't know then that I was called to be a pastor. I even told God that I wasn't a pastor. I considered myself to be strictly in the ministry of helps.

I always wondered where I got the anointing to be a pastor. One day God said to me, "Because you helped that man build his church, and you were around him, the anointing to be a pastor came on you by association."

Some of you are running after a big anointing, and you're missing the whole thing. You should determine in your heart, "Bless God, I'm going to stick with this pastor and this church." You'll be surprised. One day God will look down and say, "I can trust him. I'll put the same anointing on him."

There's something wonderful about being around men of God, where the anointing is. I'm not lifting up the flesh by stating this; I'm simply recognizing the anointing of the Spirit of God on them.

Later, when I met men of God, the Lord told me to stay close to these men, so I started working with them. Then I got around Brother Hagin, and some of his anointing rubbed off on me.

Years ago in a meeting in Hawaii, Brother Hagin laid his hands on me, and something was *imparted* to me; a stronger anointing came upon me. You see, a mantle can also be imparted by the *laying on of hands.*

Don't Get Sidetracked

And it came to pass, when the Lord would take up Elijah into heaven by a whirlwind, that Elijah went with Elisha from Gilgal.

And Elijah said unto Elisha, Tarry here, I pray thee; for the Lord hath sent me to Bethel. And Elisha said unto him, As the Lord liveth, and as thy soul liveth, I will not leave thee. So they went down to Bethel.

2 Kings 2:1,2

When you get an opportunity, study and meditate on this chapter of Second Kings; the Holy Spirit will reveal more truths to you.

Verse 1 tells us that Elijah went up into heaven "by a whirlwind"! Whirlwinds have come into a few of my services. I was taking a supernatural offering one time in Bakersfield, California, and a whirlwind came out of the balcony and down through that church. It hit all the people who were giving in that offering, and God blessed them. Oh, we need more services where a whirlwind comes from heaven and blesses the people!

From verse 2 we learn that a person has to determine in his heart that he isn't going to leave the anointing of God, no matter how hard the devil tries to get him out of the ministry. And you can be sure that the *devil will do everything he can to sidetrack you from your ministry!*

He'll sneak up beside you, like he did to me once, and ask, "What are you doing cleaning this church building?"

I answered, "I'm obeying God! Bless God, I'm not going to leave this church until a stronger anointing gets on me!"

I also remember the time I drove all the way up to Oregon to preach. I had a beat-up Buick with bald tires, and those tires seemed to talk to me all night long, saying, "You fool, you fool, you fool. . . ." Even worse, it was snowing outside, and the car heater wasn't working — no matter how much I kicked it!

The devil showed up again and said, "Why don't you quit? Why don't you quit? Why don't you quit?"

I said, "I want it too bad! I want that anointing too bad!"

I want to fellowship and walk with God so bad! I've tasted it, and I want to be part of God's plan. There are preachers who are far more capable than I am. There are silver-tongued teachers who can teach circles around me, but they don't have any meetings and I have more than I can fill, because they didn't want it bad enough. They didn't settle it in their hearts. They weren't determined.

You've got to determine in your heart when you go after something, you're going to stay with it and serve God, *no matter what*. If I hadn't determined this long ago, I would be knocked out of the race today.

Several years ago, I went through a situation where it seemed all of hell was released on me, but I remained faithful to God. Everything was taken away from me. I lost my home. God turned that situation around and gave me a better home. I lost my airplane. God gave me one that was paid for.

One day on my airplane, I looked around and said, "God, I didn't use my faith for this. Why did You give it to me?" And He said, "I'm testifying of the sacrificial giving in your life that showed you'll serve Me no matter what. You haven't seen anything yet! They'll say across the land that the hand of God is on Ed Dufresne."

That's what God did for Abel, who brought a better sacrifice than Cain; God's still testifying today, 6,000 years later, of Abel's sacrificial giving. Abel gave his best. When you give your best, God will testify of your sacrificial giving too.

Waiting on a Ministry

Too many students graduate from Bible school only to end up in their old jobs again.

For example, an airport bus driver once said to me, "I know

you! You're Brother Ed Dufresne. I heard you five years ago at Bible school, and you blessed my life."

I said, "How are you? And what are you doing now?"

He answered, "Well, I finished Bible school, but I'm 'on hold' right now, driving this bus."

Many men and women graduated with him from that same Bible school, and they're out in the ministry today. Why wasn't this man in the ministry? Something went wrong. He didn't determine in his heart to have an anointing on his life, and he fell prey to the devil.

The devil will throw anything he can in a minister's path — hardships or whatever — to try to sidetrack him and keep him from getting around the anointing. That's why many who are called into the ministry are still driving buses.

"Someday . . .," they say. But that day will never come. Now is the time to press in and give of your best! Now is the time to share the determination Elisha had for the ministry.

The Sons of the Prophets

And the sons of the prophets that were at Bethel came forth to Elisha, and said unto him, Knowest thou that the Lord will take away thy master from thy head to day? And he said, Yea, I know it; hold ye your peace.

And Elijah said unto him, Elisha, tarry here, I pray thee, for the Lord hath sent me to Jericho. And he said, As the Lord liveth, and as thy soul liveth, I will not leave thee. So they came to Jericho.

And the sons of the prophets that were at Jericho came to Elisha, and said unto him, Knowest thou that the Lord will take away thy master from thy head to day? And he answered, Yea, I know it; hold ye your peace.

2 Kings 2:3-5

Other prophets are mentioned in this story. It says they were "the sons of the prophets." I don't believe they were *physical* sons of the prophets. I believe they were prophets called by the Spirit of God, and they were being trained by prophets in schools for prophets.

At the right time, some of these sons of the prophets were so superspiritual that they knew *by the Spirit* that Elijah was about to be taken up into heaven. But my brother and sister, you can know by the Spirit of God what is about to happen and still miss it!

They said to Elisha, "Don't you know your master's going home today?" And Elisha said, "Yes, I know it. Shut your mouth. I'm staying right beside him, and before he leaves, I'm going to get his mantle" (my translation).

> *And Elijah said unto him, Tarry, I pray thee, here; for the Lord hath sent me to Jordan. And he said, As the Lord liveth, and as thy soul liveth, I will not leave thee. And they two went on.*
>
> 2 Kings 2:6

Elijah tested Elisha by deliberately trying to humiliate and discourage him. He would say, "Get away from me! Get out of here! Go on home!" But Elisha would answer, "No! As the Lord liveth, I'm going to serve you, and I'm going to stay with you" – and he wouldn't leave Elijah alone.

If we had some Elijahs today in our Bible schools, the lazy students would get upset and leave. They have it too easy. Someone else does all their praying for them. But in Elisha's life we see the kind of determination we should have. He insisted on staying by Elijah's side – *"And they two went on."*

Some of you have been floating around too long. You jump around from church to church, looking for someone to prophesy over you and push your button the right way. You've been prophesying hot air, and you won't hook up with a man of God and stick it out in his church until the anointing comes. Until you do, you won't amount to much, and you may end up shipwrecked. You ought to be getting into the Word and determining in your heart, "I will not leave the pastors of this church until the work God wants done is done in this city!"

And fifty men of the sons of the prophets went, and stood to view afar off: and they two stood by Jordan.

2 Kings 2:7

There were fifty men standing there, but only one stayed with the prophet of God and held his coat. Elisha was *determined* to get the prophet's anointing. I've heard the opinion of some Bible teachers that Elisha may have stayed with Elijah as long as twenty years.

Notice that even though the sons of the prophets were in school, they stood "afar off"! You can be in the middle of a move of God and still be "afar off." You can be "afar off" in a home meeting that is not watched over by a pastor. You can think you're a big prophet but be "afar off."

How bad do you want God to visit you? How bad do you want the anointing in your life, preachers? There are people even today who want the anointing, but they don't want it so bad they'll press in, whatever the cost. They'll say, "Oh, isn't that wonderful?" Then they'll back off, sit back, and criticize. That's what the fifty sons of the prophets did. They stood afar off and prophesied.

And that's what a certain preacher used to do to me. The devil would send him by the church I was helping build. He'd pull up to the construction site in his big, new car, playing tapes, and he'd watch us put in the foundation. Then he'd yell, "Brother Ed, what are you doing out there in that dirt? You ought to be a big-time preacher like me. Come on, man. Get out of that stuff. You've got an anointing on your life!"

But God had told me to get in that ditch and help build that church. I ran my maintenance business at night, and I went behind the Safeway store to collect day-old bread and vegetables to eat.

Like Elisha, I was determined in my heart that I was going to get an anointing on my life! I loved God too much to turn from the call.

> *And Elijah took his mantle, and wrapped it together, and smote the waters, and they were divided hither and thither, so that they two went over on dry ground.*
>
> *And it came to pass, when they were gone over, that Elijah said unto Elisha, Ask what I shall do for thee, before I be taken away from thee. And Elisha said, I pray thee, let A DOUBLE PORTION of thy spirit be upon me.*
>
> *And he said, Thou hast asked a hard thing: nevertheless, if thou see me when I am taken from thee, it shall be so unto thee; but if not, it shall not be so.*
>
> *And it came to pass, as they still went on, and talked, that, behold, there appeared a chariot of fire, and horses of fire, and parted them both asunder; and Elijah went up by a whirlwind into heaven.*
>
> *And Elisha saw it, and . . . he took up also the mantle of Elijah that fell from him. . . .*
>
> 2 Kings 2:8-13

Anointed by Association

We see from these verses that your anointing can be stronger than the person's that you've been associated with. Elisha got *a double portion* of the anointing Elijah had!

And it could happen to you! God is no respecter of persons. It doesn't matter how old or young you are. Look at Smith Wigglesworth. He was in his late forties when his ministry got going – and he shook continents for God. We're still talking about his ministry.

Years ago, Brother Wigglesworth was a speaker in a meeting in England when he heard an American by the name of Lester Sumrall preach. Afterwards, Wigglesworth went up to him and said, "Listen, young man, you need to come over to my house. I need to talk to you." Their friendship began with that first meeting.

Brother Wigglesworth would read the Word of God to Brother Sumrall and pray with him. Then he'd say, "Now, young man, I'm going to bless you." And he'd stand up and bless him.

Do you know why Dr. Sumrall was so bold? He got Smith Wigglesworth's boldness! And do you know why so many preachers took Dr. Sumrall's trips to Israel? They wanted to be around him to get his anointing!

I've been around the world with Dr. Sumrall. I've sat next to him on airplanes and in airports. He's done the same thing for me that Smith Wigglesworth did for him. He'd put his arms around me and read the Word to me. I always liked being around him, because I wanted the wisdom that man had.

Dr. Sumrall said to me one time, "Brother Ed, the tragic thing is that when these great men of God get older, none of the young men go to visit them. I know there are a lot of young men who would like to have the anointing that is on my life, but not too many want to pay the price."

God spoke to Dr. Sumrall and said, "I want you to impart the anointing that's on your life into these young men." That's why God gave Dr. Sumrall a jet. He flew all over the country to preach in churches — but he went to minister to the young pastors as well. He told me so.

Elijah told Elisha that he had asked for "a hard thing." It's a hard thing to be a prophet. (If it were easy, everyone could sit around and watch television all day, and a strong anointing would simply fall on their lives.)

Elijah added, "Nevertheless — because of your determination, and because you stayed with me even when I tried to shake you – if you see me when I am taken from you, it shall be so unto you; but if not, it shall not be so."

Elisha saw Elijah go up in the chariot of fire. Why didn't those fifty sons of the prophets see it? Because they were afar off, *playing* at being prophets.

> *He took up also the mantle of Elijah that fell from him, and went back, and stood by the bank of Jordan;*
>
> *And he took the mantle of Elijah that fell from him, and smote the waters, and said, Where is the Lord God of Elijah? and when he also had smitten the waters, they parted hither and thither: and Elisha went over.*
>
> *And when the sons of the prophets which were to view at Jericho saw him, they said, The spirit of Elijah doth rest on Elisha. And they came to meet him, and bowed themselves to the ground before him.*

And they said unto him, Behold now, there be with thy servants
fifty strong men; let them go, we pray thee, and seek thy master. . . .
                                                    2 Kings 2:13-16

The "Bless Me" Bunch

The sons of the prophets missed it, even though they were in Bible school. Why weren't they there beside Elijah, pressing in for his mantle, as Elisha was? They could have been there, but they didn't want to pay the price. They hadn't determined in their heart, "I'm going to have an anointing on my life when I come out of this school!"

They were too busy playing games, going to Charismatic meetings, and having Holy Ghost rubdowns, prophesying over one another in their "Bless Me Club"! They were saying, "You prophesy over me, and I'll prophesy over you. You prophesy that I'm great, and I'll prophesy over you that you're great!"

They wouldn't do anything to get the mantle. They wouldn't get involved. They wouldn't get around the man of God. They wouldn't offer to hold his coat. They wouldn't offer to help a pastor do anything. They wouldn't offer to clean the church toilets for Jesus.

They're the ones sitting on the back row today, waiting for the service to be over so they can pass out their business cards. They also sit at the employment office, moaning, "I don't understand it! I can't find any place to preach." Why? They weren't determined to get what they went after. (If you don't have anything to say, you aren't going to be invited to preach anyway.)

I had students like Elisha in my training center. They worked hard in the ministry of helps, got around men of God to increase their anointing, and did whatever else they could to be involved. They determined in their hearts, "Bless God, I'm not leaving until I get that anointing!"

They would ask me, "Can we hold your coat? Can we drive you to a meeting?" They wanted to get around that anointing. They did pick up the anointing that is on me, and they are in the ministry today. They have big churches. In fact, some of them have a bigger church than I had!

After Elijah was taken up into heaven in the fiery chariot, the sons of the prophets camped out in the desert for three days, searching for his body. Of course, they never found it, because his body was not in a graveyard on this earth. Elijah was so wrapped up with God, he just took off!

There are a lot of people today who are looking for dead men's anointings!

The man of God — Elisha — was there in their midst, but they went out chasing after a dead man's anointing!

Many people today are running around after dead men's anointings when there's a man of God in their own town! They ought to go and hold his coat. And if they have the ministry of making money, they ought to shovel it into his ministry.

The sons of the prophets came back worn out only to find that Elisha now had a double portion of Elijah's anointing — and he was splitting rivers and performing other miracles with that mantle!

That's what I'm after: splitting rivers! I want the power of

God. And that's what the world is looking for too — men and women who have the Holy Ghost and are full of His power.

Elisha was determined. He was hungry for that anointing. He had killed all his cattle and left everything to go and serve God. The other prophets missed it, but Elisha didn't. Elisha wanted that mantle, and he was determined to pay the price for that anointing.

Sermon 10

How To Increase Your Anointing

It pays to serve God. The Word of God works. It doesn't matter where you're at in life right now — how low you are, or how high you are — the Word never changes. You can build a house on the Word of God, and after the storms of life come and go, you will still remain. Let's look at something the Word says in Second Kings 2:1,2:

> *And it came to pass, when the Lord would take up Elijah into heaven by a whirlwind, that Elijah went with Elisha from Gilgal.*
>
> *And Elijah said unto Elisha, Tarry here, I pray thee; for the Lord hath sent me to Bethel. And Elisha said unto him, As the Lord liveth, and as thy soul liveth, I will not leave thee. So they went down to Bethel.*

I want to talk to you preachers, and also to everyday believers. If you make up your mind you're not going to leave the Lord, you'll have to forsake all.

I like the determination of Elisha. Do you preachers in full-time ministry, and you who know you're called to preach the gospel, want a stronger anointing? There's a price to pay.

I got a note from a young man who testified about coming to my services. He was in rebellion towards God. His mother was praying for him. He told me that during one of the services he ran out — he couldn't take it. But, then, he came back.

He kept coming back to our church, and then got hold of my tapes. Finally, he went up to a mountain, gave his heart to Jesus, got turned on to the Word of God, and forsook his friends.

They told him, "You're crazy; you're getting to be a fanatic. We want to go out and drink beer with you, but we don't want you to talk about Jesus."

He got hold of the Word of God, and I noticed something about this young man. There was a strong anointing on his life. Many times he'd sit in my office and want me to tell him things, but I wouldn't tell him. Sometimes he'd want me to give him money, but if I had done that, I'd have been his source.

A lot of young men have come and a lot have left and gotten mad at me. Now they're in the dump heap of life. You've got to make a determination in your heart to serve God, no matter what it costs. And you've got to determine to get that anointing, whatever it costs.

This young man was around me and in my church. And he said, "Bless God, I want that anointing. I want that ministry. I want to get involved." Many times he'd get mad, but he'd keep coming back.

Do you really want something from God? How bad do you want it? I can count, in the natural, the things it has cost me to serve God. You can come to a point in life when even loved ones will forsake you, because they want to do the things of the world. They'll use other excuses, but really, they want to go into the world. They don't want to serve God.

I've seen the devil even get loved ones to come to a person and try to get him to back off from what God told him to do.

Obedience Demands Action

Let's notice something again from our text:

> And Elijah said unto Elisha, Tarry here, I pray thee; for the
> Lord hath sent me to Bethel. And Elisha said unto him, As the Lord
> liveth, and as thy soul liveth, I will not leave thee. So they went down
> to Bethel.

2 Kings 2:2

It says Elisha *"went"* to Bethel. He had to forsake everything.

When God spoke to Abraham in Genesis 12, He said, "Come out of that country." Abraham lived in a rich city. As a matter of fact, the sewers were lined with cobblestones. That's a nice sewer! And God told Abraham to come out and live in a tent.

I can hear Sarah right now: "Well, I have a nice home, I have a washing machine and other things, and I don't know if I want to serve God that much." But I thank God she went with him.

I thank God Abraham went too. It could have been the other way around. What if Sarah had said, "I'm going to do what God told me to do," and Abraham had wanted to stay with the nice things?

I want you to know, the world wants you. Satan will pay a lot of money to get you, especially when you're determined to get something from God. How bad do you want it? If you haven't made up your mind, you may wonder why you don't get your healing or don't get blessed. How bad do you want God to come into your house, and the glory of God to be in your home?

Elisha said, "I'm not leaving you, prophet of God. I'm going to stay right with you."

Don't Stand on the Sidelines

So Elijah and Elisha went down to Bethel.

> *And the sons of the prophets that were at Bethel came forth to Elisha, and said unto him, Knowest thou that the Lord will take away thy master from thy head to day? And he said, Yea, I know it; hold ye your peace.*
>
> 2 Kings 2:3

In other words, he said, "Shut up!" Now, these prophets were in the school of the prophets, and it was revealed to them Elijah was going to be taken away. But notice one man by the name of Elisha. These other prophets could have received what he got.

> *And Elijah said unto him, Elisha, tarry here, I pray thee; for the Lord hath sent me to Jericho. And he said, As the Lord liveth, and as thy soul liveth, I will not leave thee. So they came to Jericho.*
>
> 2 Kings 2:4

Here's what those at the school of the prophets said:

> *And the sons of the prophets that were at Jericho came to Elisha, and said unto him, Knowest thou that the Lord will take away thy master from thy head to day? And he answered, Yea, I know it; hold ye your peace.*
>
> *And Elijah said unto him, Tarry, I pray thee, here; for the Lord hath sent me to Jordan. And he said, As the Lord liveth, and as thy soul liveth, I will not leave thee. And they two went on.*
>
> 2 Kings 2:5,6

Notice the different cities they went to. Those at the school of the prophets were standing on the side, watching all this.

Be Determined

I'm determined enough, if I had been on the sidelines and seen that the anointing was about to fall, I'd have been in there with Elisha. I've always been that way. I want everything God gives.

Somebody once asked me, "Why did God anoint you? Why have miracles happened in your life? Why you?"

Well, why me? Really, in the natural, I have no kind of education, per se. I don't have any natural ability to speak in public. In school, I couldn't even get up in front of the class to talk. When I was president of the car club, I couldn't get up to receive a trophy. And after I got saved, I couldn't give a testimony because of a fear of people.

I asked God, "Why me?" And He said, "Because you've got the determination to serve Me."

Some won't serve God because of circumstances. They'll serve Him when everything is going fine, but if they lose everything, something happens to their determination. There is a price to be paid for the anointing.

A lot of people say, "I want it!" But they don't want to pay the price. Elisha said, "No, I'm not leaving you. I'm going with you." He had to forsake everything to do it.

Pursue the Anointing

Let's look at Second Kings 2:7:

And fifty men of the sons of the prophets went, and stood to view afar off: and they two stood by Jordan.

Now, isn't this amazing? These other prophets were afar off. I can see them hiding behind the trees, saying, "What's

233

really going to happen here?" There are always people standing off to the side of the supernatural, saying, "Oh" and "Ah," and "What are you going to do now?"

But notice one man said, "I'm not letting you out of my sight."

I remember when Brother Hagin laid hands on me. There is an anointing by association. If these other prophets had gotten on the ball, they could have been around Elijah.

But there was one by the name of Elisha who determined in his heart he was going to get what he went after.

I remember I said, "Lord, whatever Brother Hagin has, I want that. I want to be around those men." And the Lord has opened doors for me to associate with them.

If you're willing to pay the price, you can get impartations from another man's anointing. Young men who have been around me pick up traits with which the Lord has anointed me. And that's not copying.

Many pick up part of a man's anointing and they carry it. Brother Hagin himself says there are some ministries he doesn't do anymore, because young men have been around him and picked these things up.

Do you want a miracle? Do you want a stronger anointing on your life? Listen to what the Spirit of the Lord is saying in our text:

> *And Elijah took his mantle, and wrapped it together, and smote the waters, and they were divided hither and thither, so that they two went over on dry ground.*
>
> 2 Kings 2:8

How would you like to have that anointing?

And it came to pass, when they were gone over, that Elijah said unto Elisha, Ask what I shall do for thee, before I be taken away from thee. And Elisha said, I pray thee, let a double portion of thy spirit be upon me.

And he said, Thou hast asked a hard thing. . . .

2 Kings 2:9,10

This indicates to me it's a hard thing to get another man's anointing, or a stronger anointing on you. But notice what Elijah said: *"Nevertheless. . . ."*

You know, if it were easy, every tinhorn preacher would have a strong anointing on his life. But there aren't enough preachers willing to pay the price. They want nice cars and nice homes, but they don't want to pay the price to get that anointing.

Brother Hagin traveled around in an old, broken-down car for years before he actually saw a manifestation of faith operating.

Faith preachers today have it easy compared to men of a few years ago. Some of those men faced great hardships, yet they kept confessing the Word of God.

We have started churches overnight. It's taken other men twenty years to do what we're doing now in three or four years. But this is because those men sacrificed and paid the price. It's a hard thing.

And he said, Thou hast asked a hard thing: nevertheless, if thou see me when I am taken from thee, it shall be so unto thee; but if not, it shall not be so.

2 Kings 2:10

Don't Be a Quitter

God told me one night, "There's a quality in you — you just don't know how to quit. You might fall down, and you might lie there for a while, but you'll get back up and go right on. And you determine in your heart, 'I'm not going to leave until I get that anointing.'"

Some young preachers today go across town and gripe if they receive a small offering. They say, "I can't even buy a hot dog with that!"

They want to start out by renting a hall at the Holiday Inn. But when only twenty people show up, they get upset and throw their Bible down.

They have asked a hard thing. God doesn't give His mantles to every tinhorn preacher who comes along. People are going to have to prove to God they're worthy of the anointing.

The fifty prophets had the same opportunity as Elisha. But they wanted to stay in their nice, comfortable school and prophesy to each other.

One prophet went after the man of God and it cost him. The other fifty were saying, "You're following that man and he's going to go home and be with the Lord. What are you following him for?" They stayed in the safety of their little school. But one man went after the hard thing.

Ministries don't come easy. Do you want everything handed to you? You're going to have to go after it. Things get a little rough and people gripe.

Pull the Anointing Out

Did you know you can pull the gift out of a prophet by putting a demand on that gift?

I was at an ordination service one time and there were a thousand people at the meeting.

Those in charge of the meeting kept saying, "Now Ed's right here. He's a prophet. Ed, do you have something to say?"

I said, "No, no, no, no." And I just sat back. I didn't want to get involved. But they kept pulling on the gift.

Finally, the power of God knocked me out of my chair and we started praying for the sick. People were lying all over. It was a miraculous service because they put a demand on the gift.

Elisha put a demand on Elijah.

Elijah said, "You go and leave me alone."

But Elisha said, "No, I'm not going to leave you alone — I'm going to stay right with you." Elisha wouldn't quit.

A Lesson from Experience

I remember a time when my family and I had almost no food in the ice box. My kids hardly had any clothes. And yet I got in my old, broken-down Buick, and drove in the snow to preach to a handful of people.

The church was in Burns, Oregon. That's out in the desert. I was supposed to have a big crusade and only a handful of people showed up.

I was in the prophet's quarters — I didn't have the money to get a motel. They put me in the attic of the church.

The winds were blowing through the rafters, and those winds were saying, "You're an idiot, you're an idiot, you're an idiot. What are you doing here?"

Halfway through the meeting, I phoned home and told my family, "I'm quitting the ministry."

I put the phone down and God said, "You big quitter, you. Here I give you a meeting and you're ready to quit halfway through it."

The meeting had been going on for a week. I said, "Nobody is showing up." He replied, "What do you care?"

Numbers, numbers, numbers — we ought to come out of the book of Numbers and go into the book of Acts.

I've seen young preachers come out of Bible school and get mad because they weren't big successes overnight.

Ministry or Money?

I've had people say, "The Lord told me to come work for you, but you're supposed to give me a certain amount a month. You've got to promise me that."

If they're not willing to believe God for their finances, though, they really don't want to be a part of the ministry.

I tell them, "Go wash dishes. Go to work. You really don't want it."

Elisha wanted it.

Elisha's Request

And it came to pass, when they were gone over, that Elijah said unto Elisha, Ask what I shall do for thee, before I be taken away from thee. And Elisha said, I pray thee, let a double portion of thy spirit be upon me.

238

And he said, Thou hast asked a hard thing: Nevertheless, if thou see me when I am taken from thee, it shall be so unto thee; but if not, it shall not be so.

And it came to pass, as they still went on, and talked, that, behold, there appeared a chariot of fire, and horses of fire, and parted them both asunder; and Elijah went by a whirlwind into heaven.

And Elisha saw it, and he cried, My father, my father. . . .

2 Kings 2:9-12

Remember, those other fifty prophets could have gotten in on this. But they were in their comfortable school. They had a comfortable place to stay; they didn't want to follow an old, beat-up preacher around. They didn't want to sleep outside. They didn't want to leave their comfortable dorm.

They were saying, "Ha, ha, ha, what are you going to do now, Elisha? Your master is going to heaven. You ought to get over here with us."

But Elisha was more interested in the anointing that was on that old prophet. I've seen a lot of young men come and work for me, and I've seen a lot of them go — and I've wept.

I've said, "They won't make it. They're not willing to pay the price." They want me to pay them a big, fat salary so they can have a nice, beautiful home.

Receiving the New Cloak

And Elisha saw it, and he cried, My father, my father, the chariot of Israel, and the horsemen thereof. And he saw him no more: and he took hold of his own clothes, and rent them in two pieces.

2 Kings 2:12

Notice, he took his clothes off. He was getting ready for a new anointing. That's faith. He didn't have it yet, but he took his old clothes off, getting ready for his new cloak.

239

You see, the anointing is like a coat, or cloak. There are times that coat will come on me, and I can see what's wrong with people. Then there are times that coat will lift, and it won't work. At those times I might as well just go on with the laying on of hands.

We have miracles in our meetings all across the nation because of the anointing. A girl who was doing sign language while I was preaching now has a normal back. The devil was beating her over the head, saying, "You're deformed." But she's not deformed anymore. Why? The coat came on me and I saw what was wrong. Her shoulders moved and God straightened her back.

The Prophets' Mistake

> He took up also the mantle of Elijah that fell from him, and went back, and stood by the bank of the Jordan [notice, Elisha put the anointing right to work];
>
> And he took the mantle of Elijah that fell from him, and smote the waters, and said, Where is the Lord God of Elijah? and when he also had smitten the waters, they parted hither and thither: and Elisha went over.
>
> And when the sons of the prophets which were to view at Jericho saw him, they said, The spirit of Elijah doth rest on Elisha. And they came to meet him, and bowed themselves to the ground before him.
>
> And they said unto him, Behold now, there be with thy servants fifty strong men; let them go, we pray thee, and seek thy master; lest peradventure the Spirit of the Lord hath taken him up, and cast him upon some mountain, or into some valley. And he said, Ye shall not send.
>
> And when they urged him till he was ashamed, he said, Send. They sent therefore fifty men; and they sought three days, but found him not.
>
> 2 Kings 2:13-17

Those fifty were unbelieving prophets. They wanted the anointing, but they didn't get it. I've had people say, "Yes, we're behind you, Brother Ed." But when the pressure hit, they scattered. They didn't want to pay the price.

At first people see the glory. They see the anointing on you. They say, "Brother Ed, we want what you've got."

But I've seen them come around my ministry – I've seen some of them grab it and run with it, but they ran too early and they got down the road and it waned. They didn't stick with it. They didn't go from city to city with the man of God and do what the man of God, by the Spirit, told them to do.

Do you know what they really wanted? They just wanted the anointing for their own glory. If you just want it for your own glory, so you can be a big shot, you might as well forget it. It will wane quickly. You must use it to get people's needs met.

You see, those prophets didn't want to pay the price. But after they saw the anointing on Elisha, they ran out to get it. By that time, he was already gone.

Paying All

I've had people around me who said they were my friends. But they didn't want to pay the price. When tragedy knocked at my door, they said, "We love you, brother, but God is calling us somewhere else."

I've had other ministers criticize me. They wanted the anointing I had, but they didn't want to pay the price. Some just wanted to play church.

And ministers —— don't tell me you want to pay the price if you aren't willing to fast and get in the presence of God before meetings. You can't sit around and eat like a pig all day long, and then minister.

There are some who could have had the anointing Brother Hagin has, but they didn't want to pay the price. Yet others stayed right with him and carried his coat. They saw him as human when he acted like a human. But they didn't look on that. They looked at the anointing on his life.

There were fifty-one prophets, and one made a decision, "I'm not going to leave you."

The others were on the sidelines, seeing if anything was going to happen.

The key to an increased anointing in your life is this: *You must be willing to pay all!*

Sermon 11

How To Activate Miracles

God spoke up to me and said, "Tell My people to declare the power they have with Me, that He who is within them is greater than he who is in the world." (1 John 4:4.)

God wants you to know that *you* have power with *Him*, and He wants you to *tell the people!!!*

Jesus' Ministry

> *The Spirit of the Lord is upon me, because he hath anointed me to preach the gospel to the poor; he hath sent me to heal the brokenhearted, to preach deliverance to the captives, and recovering of sight to the blind, to set at liberty them that are bruised, to preach the acceptable year of the Lord.*
>
> *And he closed the book, and he gave it again to the minister, and sat down. And the eyes of all them that were in the synagogue were fastened on him.*
>
> Luke 4:18-20

Jesus told the people that He was anointed of God. Everywhere He went, Jesus told the people that He was anointed of God. There's a reason. There is a law here that we need to learn. He told the people who He was and what He was doing; if He didn't tell them, then faith wouldn't come. *"Faith cometh by hearing, and hearing by the word of God"* (Romans 10:17). And, if we don't tell the world who we are in Christ, how are they to know?

243

Many people who are in false cults today are persistent about their beliefs. We need to be the same way concerning the gospel. We ought to be as bold as they are. No, *even bolder!* The "bold bunch," as Kenneth Hagin says.

The Bible says in Philippians 2:7,8 that Jesus of Nazareth stripped Himself of all divine privileges as the Son of God. It didn't say that He was not the Son of God, but that He didn't walk as the Son of God, with divine privileges from heaven. He came on this earth and walked as a man, under the Old Covenant. He quoted Scripture, saying, "It is written." He didn't go around saying, "I'm the Son of God. Get your healing today."

Jesus was a preacher. He walked as an Old Testament prophet. He was the Son of God, but He didn't use that power. *He used the Word of God!!!*

My life was changed when I found out that Jesus walked as a man.

I had been raised as a Catholic. I was born again when I was twenty-five years old. I used to think to myself, *If Jesus would only appear to me, I'll really receive my healing.* But I found out that He came down here as a man. He walked on the face of this earth and used the Old Covenant and lived in victory! He has appeared to us already. We can receive our healing now by faith.

It would have been unfair for Jesus to have used His divine privileges here on earth. He had to come down as a man and go through the same tests as you and I; but, I'll tell you this. He passed every one of them. He passed them by using the Word of God and so can we!

Satan took Jesus to the pit of hell because all of the sins of the world were laid on Him. Jesus Himself was a man without sin. Satan said, "I've got You now," but God said, "That's enough!" Satan answered, "What are You talking about, 'That's enough'?" God said, "You have Him down there illegally. He is a man without sin." And God raised Jesus from the dead.

We Have Power

The Bible calls the devil our adversary. "Adversary" in the Greek language means "lawsuitor" (opponent in a lawsuit). The devil is running around trying to put a lawsuit on you, just like he tried to do with Jesus. But when we're walking according to the Word, there are no legal grounds for Satan to stand on.

When we have on our helmet of salvation and breastplate of righteousness and all the rest of the armor of God that He provides for us (Ephesians 6:13-17), the devil looks at us and he sees Jesus, and he knows he's fighting a losing battle.

The Bible says to humble ourselves under the mighty hand of God (1 Peter 5:6). Do you know what a humble man really is?

The Lord showed me that a humble man is a man who will take counsel from someone else. An egotist, you see, won't take anybody's word but their own; a humble man will take counsel from another.

When you take your own word about yourself, your

circumstances, your body, or your checkbook, you're being an egotist. You're being humble about your situation when you take counsel from God's Word, saying, "My God meets all my needs according to His riches in glory by Christ Jesus" (Philippians 4:19). Or, "By His stripes we were healed" (1 Peter 2:24).

The world has twisted things around so much that we think we're being humble when, in reality, we're being egotists, taking the word of the situation instead of the Word of God. The Bible doesn't say that we're not to be exalted, just that we're not to exalt ourselves.

First Peter 5:6 goes on to say, *"Humble yourselves therefore under the mighty hand of God, that He may exalt you in due time."*

He wants you exalted, but He'll do it. Just humble yourself to His Word and He'll exalt you in due time, right on time. He will exalt us out of problems, sickness, and poverty.

The world needs to know that we, as Christians, have God's Word to use on this earth. God has given us the power of attorney, the legal right to use His Name and expect to get the same results that Jesus would get.

If I give someone the power of attorney so that they can conduct my business in my absence, they can sign my name and it is just as valid and binding as if I had signed it myself. Christians are one with Christ, and we have the same authority in the Name of Jesus as Jesus Himself. In His Name we shall cast out demons. In His Name we shall pray for the sick and they shall recover. In His Name even greater things shall we do. But, the world will never know unless we tell them!

246

The woman with the issue of blood had *heard* of Jesus (Mark 5:25-27). In verse 28 she said, *"If I may touch but his clothes, I shall be whole."*

In verse 29 she touched the garment Jesus was wearing, and *"... straightway the fountain of her blood was dried up; and she felt in her body that she was healed of that plague."*

This case involved special anointings. This lady had faith that if she but touched Jesus' garment, she would be made whole. She had *heard* about Jesus and her faith arose. Her faith is what got her healed, not Jesus being the Son of God. Jesus Himself said, *"Thy faith hath made thee whole"* (Mark 5:34). He felt the healing virtue pass from His body when she applied her faith and touched Him.

When the world hears about us, that we have the power of God, they, too, will have faith and receive. If a man were to walk silently down a street, no one would know who he was. Certainly no one would come running up to him to jerk on his suit to receive a healing. No one would bring their sickbed to the street so that this man's shadow might pass over them.

But if he told them who he was *in Christ* and the power that he had *in the Name of Jesus,* they could apply their faith and be healed.

Acts 3:1-4 says:

Now Peter and John went up together into the temple at the hour of prayer, being the ninth hour.

And a certain man lame from his mother's womb was carried, whom they laid daily at the gate of the temple which is called Beautiful, to ask alms of them that entered into the temple;

Who seeing Peter and John about to go into the temple, asked an alms.

> *And Peter, fastening his eyes upon him with John, said, Look on us.*

He said, "Look on us." Look on us. He did not say, "Look on us; I prayed for three short legs today, so look at me." He's not saying that. He is saying, "Look on us. We've got something for you — *He who is within us*" (1 John 4:4).

Acts 3:5 says, *"And he gave heed unto them, expecting to receive something of them."*

This man would have never given heed to them if Peter hadn't said something. He said, "Look on us." Then Peter said:

> *Silver and gold have I none; but such as I have give I thee: In the name of Jesus Christ of Nazareth rise up and walk.*
>
> *And he took him by the right hand, and lifted him up: and immediately his feet and ankle bones received strength.*
>
> Acts 3:6,7

In the Name of Jesus that man rose up. Peter had the Name of Jesus. I have the Name of Jesus. You've got the Name of Jesus!

The Word says for you to lay hands on the sick, and they will recover. You don't need special anointings. You have the Name of Jesus. But you have got to tell the people so they can believe.

It Takes Faith

God wants you made whole, but He can't force it upon you against your will. You've got to *believe* it and *receive* it by faith.

In Mark 16:15-18 Jesus said:

> *And he said unto them, Go ye into all the world, and preach the gospel to every creature.*

> *He that believeth and is baptized shall be saved; but he that believeth not shall be damned.*
>
> *And these signs shall follow them that believe; In my name shall they cast out devils; they shall speak with new tongues;*
>
> *They shall take up serpents; and if they drink any deadly thing, it shall not hurt them; they shall lay hands on the sick, and they [the sick] shall recover.*

It says that these signs shall follow them that believe. Are you a believer? I used to say, "Well, these signs are following you."

I preached that one night and afterward in the back room, God said, "You are wrong about what you preached from Mark 16." I said, "What are You talking about? It says right here in my Bible that these signs shall follow them that believe." He said, "You said that those signs are following believers, all born-again believers." I said, "That's right, that's what You said." He said, "No, I said that the signs would follow them that *believe*; if they believe that the signs will follow them, the signs will follow them."

Do you see what I'm saying? There are many born-again Christians (believers) who don't *believe* in healing. They do *believe* in salvation. They'll fight you over that. But healing? They say that it has passed away.

They believe in salvation, so salvation will follow them. They don't believe in healing, so healing won't follow them. The signs will follow only those who will *believe*.

I believe in healing, so healing follows me. I believe that when I lay hands on the sick they will recover, so *they do recover.*

I want you to notice here the word "recover." How many of you have had an operation and stayed in the hospital while you recovered? Sometimes healing is a process. The devil may try to talk you out of a healing while, all the time, you are *recovering*.

Once, as I was walking from a meeting, a man came running after me, saying, "I didn't get my healing. Will you pray for me again?" I told him, "You are *recovering*."

There are times when healings are instantaneous, and there are times when people are recovering as they go out the door. If you've been prayed for, you should say, "Praise God! A man of God laid hands on me and I'm recovering!"

You should not look to the circumstances (and be an egotist), but to the Word of God (and be humble). God is exalting you out of sickness. You are recovering! Jesus spoke to the fig tree and it dried up, not right at that moment, but it dried up from the roots (Mark 11:14-20).

Mark 6:54-56 says:

> *And when they were come out of the ship, straightway they knew him,*
>
> *And ran through that whole region round about, and began to carry about in beds those that were sick, where they heard he was.*
>
> *And whithersoever he entered, into villages, or cities, or country, they laid the sick in the streets, and besought him that they might touch if it were but the border of his garment: and as many as touched him were made whole.*

Why did all those sick folks want to be carried out into the street as this man walked by? Jesus didn't say, "I'm the Son of God. Look at Me." He didn't say, "My being the Son of God is what will heal you." Or, "My special anointing is what will make you whole." He told the woman with the issue of blood that her faith had made her whole (Mark 5:34). It was her faith in that special anointing. Faith must have come to these people, and it must have come by hearing.

Matthew 14:34-36 says:

> *And when they were gone over, they came into the land of Gennesaret.*
>
> *And when the men of that place had knowledge of him, they sent out into all that country round about, and brought unto him all that were diseased;*
>
> *And besought him that they might only touch the hem of his garment: and as many as touched [it] were made perfectly whole.*

Go back to verse 35, where we read, *"And when the men of that place had knowledge of him. . . ."* It says that they had *knowledge* of Him. Somebody must have *told* them about Jesus, and *faith* came by *hearing.*

In Luke 6:17-19 we read:

> *And he came down with them, and stood in the plain, and the company of his disciples, and a great multitude of people out of all Judea and Jerusalem, and from the sea coast of Tyre and Sidon, which came to hear him, and to be healed of their diseases;*
>
> *And they that were vexed with unclean spirits: and they were healed.*
>
> *And the whole multitude sought to touch him: for there went virtue out of him, and healed them all.*

Healing virtue, a power, went out of Jesus. It wasn't just because He was the Son of God, mind you. It was because God anointed Him.

Would God have to anoint the Son? Wouldn't He already have been anointed? Wasn't He the Anointed One? God had to anoint Him for His earthly ministry. How did God anoint Jesus? With the Holy Ghost and with power (Acts 10:38).

God had to anoint Jesus so He could get His job done here on the earth (John 17:4). He didn't come on the scene in a dress, holding a lamb, saying, "Here I am. Get your healing today." No, He had to preach to the people. He had to *tell* them. Some people didn't believe Him and tried to push Him off a cliff, tried to kill Him. He had to *tell* the people that God had anointed Him, so that they could believe. He had to *tell* them.

Personal Examples

I'll never forget the first "big" healing service that I had. I knew that God had called me to preach to 5,000 people that night. Only two showed up. TWO! I said, "Oh, Lord, You called me to minister and only two showed up! Only TWO showed up!"

God spoke to me and said, "What do you care if there are 5,000 or two? Just get out there and preach the Word. If I can trust you with two, then I can trust you with a hundred, then five hundred, then thousands."

So I stopped being an egotist, and humbled myself to God and preached the Word. And the two got healed. One hundred percent success! God wants to use us where we are. He'll exalt us as we humble ourselves to Him.

The power of the living God is present now, and we can release it by laying hands on the sick. God said, "The reason the world isn't bringing the bedfast out, the reason they're not bringing the sick over to your house, the reason they're not phoning you to pray for them is because you haven't *told* them that you've got power with God."

You tell the people! Faith cometh by hearing, and hearing by the Word of God. They'll never know that you've got power with God unless you *tell* them so. They might tell you that you're being egotistical about it, but when they get sick, they'll call you up.

Mark 7:32,33,35 says:

> *And they bring unto him one that was deaf, and had an impediment in his speech; and they beseech him to put his hand upon him.*
>
> *And he took him aside from the multitude, and put his fingers into his ears . . .*
>
> *And straightway his ears were opened. . . .*

Jesus appeared to me in October 1977 and told me to stick my fingers in people's ears as I prayed for their hearing. Across this nation we have seen almost 100 percent success in people's ears opening up.

It's Time for You To Use the Power of God

In John 14:12-14 Jesus said:

> *Verily, verily, I say unto you* [in other words, "Truly, really, I'm telling you the truth"], *he that believeth on me, the works that I do shall he do also; and greater works than these shall he do* [that's talking to YOU]; *because I go unto my Father.*
>
> *And whatsoever ye shall ask in my name, that will I do, that the Father may be glorified in the Son.*
>
> *If ye shall ask any thing in my name, I will do it.*

I want to say it one more time. I just can't say it enough. God said for me to tell the people – that's YOU – to tell the world that *you've* got power with God. *You* will lay hands on the sick and they will recover. Whatsoever *you* shall ask in His name, He will do it.

You ought to have your phone number put on a little card and give it to people, saying, "When you need healing, give me a call." They'll remember that. Then, after you get them healed, you can win them to the Lord. Miracles are the "dinner bell" for salvation.

Remember, God said for you to *tell the people* who you are in Him.

> But ye shall receive power, after that the Holy Ghost is come upon you: and ye shall be witnesses unto Me both in Jerusalem, and in all Judea, and in Samaria, and unto the uttermost part of the earth.
>
> Acts 1:8

Do you know what witnesses are? The dictionary describes a "witness" as something serving as evidence or proof."

You are the evidence, *you* are the proof that God heals today. You're the proof-producers. You're the evidence. The carnal-minded don't know. *You've* got to tell them and be their evidence!

Tell the people!

Part IV
Healing Testimonies

God Recreates Thirty-Eight Inches of Intestines

I was born in July 1969 and had been sick from that day. When I was three months old the doctors thought that I had bad colic; however, I began running a fever for ten days on six-week intervals.

From that point until I was three years old, I developed other symptoms of vomiting, diarrhea, and mouth ulcers. On top of all these symptoms, I had periodic bouts of bronchitis which in one case turned into pneumonia.

In October 1972, I was hospitalized for five weeks and almost died twice. Once from the pneumonia and the second time from the disease.

Unable to diagnose the disease, I was discharged on cortisone drugs and a diagnosis of fever from an unknown origin.

As I was slowly taken off the medication, I became sick again and was admitted to a hospital in Houston for tests in July 1973.

After two weeks, I was diagnosed with juvenile rheumatoid arthritis and discharged on more medication.

Three weeks later, I had high fevers and became extremely sick and had to be rushed back to Houston for emergency surgery in August. They removed thirty inches of intestine that had ruptured in ten places.

The surgeon said to my parents that he did nothing to save me but that there was a God in heaven who wanted me alive. The Lord brought me through it but I was diagnosed with Crohn's disease a week later.

I did well from then until the spring of 1977 when I

contracted mononucleosis for nine weeks. After that the Crohn's became active again. I had gotten progressively worse until September 1979. The doctor told my parents I was inoperable and if increasing my medicine didn't work I was going to die.

The next day a Baptist minister anointed me with oil and we claimed James 5:14,15 for my life. I improved dramatically overnight but still had to have surgery in January of 1980 to remove eight more inches of obstructed intestine.

We continued to believe for my healing and stood on God's Word. Over the next five years God worked in my life and my health slowly manifested itself. In that time, I was healed of rheumatoid arthritis and steroid cataracts that I had as a result of taking so much cortisone. My growth was stunted as well.

Finally, in March 1985 you had a healing service in my church. That night God crossed the "t" in my health by recreating thirty-eight inches of *brand new* intestine.

Six months later, in the hospital for tests, my parents and I saw bewildered doctors and a clump of intestines in my belly that had not been in previous X-rays of the same area.

In August 1987 my doctor released me, saying, "Hopefully you will never have any more problems." This might not sound like much, but he had already agreed to see me until one of us died and he fully expected it.

Thank You, God, for my life.

K. A. A.
Sulphur, Louisiana

Thirty-Two Spots of Cancer Healed

On Labor Day 1999, while I was driving home from Pensacola, Florida, I felt excruciating pain in the upper part of my stomach. When I arrived home, the pain got worse.

I was admitted to the hospital to have a biopsy done. Fourteen days after the biopsy, the doctors told me that I had terminal cancer with three months to live.

A couple months following this diagnosis, you came to preach at my church. I was sitting in the front row during the service. While you were preaching, you said, "Someone in here has cancer." You were standing right beside me when you said it.

You said, "Come here! You've been told you have only three months to live."

Then you laid hands on me and I felt the power of God flow through my body. I believed that I had received my healing.

I had a doctor's appointment shortly after you prayed for me. I told the doctor that I had been healed. I asked him to give me another test.

The doctor's response was, "You and your family have been through enough. I am not going to give you another CAT scan."

I prayed and asked God to speak to the doctors so they would agree to give me another test.

I made another appointment with a cancer doctor. He said that I needed to have chemotherapy. I asked him to give me another test. He then proceeded to leave my hospital room.

When he returned to my room, he told me that he would agree to give me another test.

On December 9, 1999, he gave me another CAT scan.

On December 10, 1999, the doctor came into my hospital room smiling and said, "The thirty-two spots of cancer that were on your liver are *all* completely gone!"

Hallelujah! I just can't stop thanking God enough. I'm a thirty-two-year-old mother of three and have been healed. Thank you for doing God's work and believing He's still in the healing business.

S. S.

Iowa Creek, Alabama

Spirit of Death Leaves

On Monday night, April 27th, you prayed for a lady in a wheelchair with an oxygen apparatus. Her health had been declining for several months and she had lost sixty-three pounds.

She had had a gastronomy tube put in her that Monday morning to feed her because she could no longer eat or drink on her own without choking.

She inquired of several doctors and underwent a variety of tests, but all to no avail. Nothing could be found as to the reason for her sickness. Monday night, you prayed for her and commanded the spirit of death to leave her body.

When I spoke with her on Tuesday morning, she said that she felt that spirit leave her body as soon as you commanded it to leave. Looking at her on Tuesday, she looked like a different person. Her countenance had totally changed. Her eyes had life in them again and her smile returned. She no longer looked like the same person who went up for prayer the night before who had no hope.

Praise God she has new hope.

N. H.

Miracle Babies

My husband and I had gone to several fertility doctors and had taken medication for quite some time. I was even pregnant and had a miscarriage.

We were on a waiting list to begin another program in order to try and get pregnant, this being over the course of six and a half years.

I had gone to the doctors that very day, it was the Tuesday night of Fresh Oil 1991 and you called for anyone who was faced with something that the doctors would call incurable. With all the problems that I had been having trying to get pregnant, they weren't really giving me any hope.

So many thoughts were racing through my head, but I said I have enough faith to trust in the man of God as my point of contact and know that when he lays hands on me that the healing power of God is going to make a change in my body and so I went up and stood in line.

I released my faith when hands were being laid on me and one month later, I was pregnant without any help from the doctors. It was a miracle from God! We now have a wonderful seven-year-old son and a three-year-old son.

S. M.

Menifee, California

Knee Healed

My son had surgery on his knee not too long ago. The doctors couldn't seem to sew his knee up properly and as a result, he was unable to bend it after having the surgery. He also experienced a lot of pain with it.

My son and I attended one of your meetings and when you were praying for people, my son and I went forward. You laid hands on both of us and we went down under the power of God.

My son said, "Mom! Mom! Something's going on. I can feel something in my leg. I can stomp my leg on the floor and it doesn't hurt.

When we arrived home, we found that my son's knee was sewed back together properly, except for a tiny spot. And he is now able to bend his knee again.

M. M.

Oklahoma City, Oklahoma

No More Leg Braces

When I was a baby, my hip bone wasn't properly in its socket and as a result, I had to wear braces on my legs for two years. This problem also caused me to experience a lot of back trouble.

I was in one of your Jesus the Healer Crusades and went forward for prayer. You prayed for me and laid your hands on my legs. I felt my right leg stretching out.

I was healed! Since this time, I have not had *any* pain.

The Lord not only healed my hip, but He also healed me from oppression that I've had for many years. I am a righteous woman in the Lord, a new creature in Christ!

D. C.

Torrance, California

Receives an Overhaul

For twenty years I was in excruciating pain due to my stooped back. I also limped when I walked because I didn't have any cartilage in my hips. I was scheduled for an operation to try and correct these problems. I also suffered from arthritis.

I attended your meeting in Minnesota. You preached a dynamic message and then prayed for people. I went forward for prayer and you laid hands on me. I had faith that Jesus would heal me and He did!

I received a miracle! I am now without pain, my stooped back is straight, I don't limp anymore, and the difficulty I had in trying to move my hips is gone. I can now move with ease. I was also healed of arthritis.

The operation that I was supposed to have is no longer necessary. Glory to God!

L. T.

Minnesota

Receives New Eardrum

As a small child I suffered from double-mastoids. I had to have both eardrums punctured and both mastoid bones surgically removed, which resulted in approximately a 90 percent loss of hearing in my left ear. This was due to a lack of antibiotics.

You came to Oklahoma to hold a seminar. You called out for those who had experienced hearing loss or hearing problems to come forward for prayer.

I went forward. When you ministered to me, you stuck your fingers in my ears just as Jesus did in the Bible. While you were praying for me, I was keenly aware of movement in my inner ear.

I went down under the power of God and laid on the floor for some time. When I finally got up, I was aware of sounds that I had not been able to hear before. God healed me!

On a recent missionary trip to Guatemala, I was working in a jungle clinic with a doctor. I asked him to check my ears and much to his surprise, when he examined my left ear, he found that I had two eardrums, one old and scarred, the other new and pink, as a baby's ear. Praise God, I am healed!

B. L.

Tulsa, Oklahoma

Leg Grows

I was involved in an accident in 1971, and as a result of this accident, my right leg did not continue to grow normally as my left leg did.

On August 15, 1979, I gave birth to my son and since then, my right leg, hip, and thigh have hurt continuously.

I attended a meeting you held in Tennessee. You were ministering to people and while you were ministering to them, I believed that in Jesus' Name I would receive my healing.

As I sat there in the chair, I felt my leg grow out about one and a half inches. I have had no pain and I feel like a brand new person.

I praise God for your ministry. God bless you!

T. A.

Knoxville, Tennessee

Scoliosis Healed

My spinal cord had twisted itself over the years. I was diagnosed with having scoliosis in four different places along my spinal column, accompanied with bone spurs.

I attended one of your meetings and you called me out during the service. As you laid hands on me, I felt an intense heat and pressure, along the length of my spine. I then felt my spine being lengthened. Immediately, I was able to hold myself up with no discomfort.

The next morning I had none of the usual lower back pain or stiffness that was normally present. I attempted to bend back and forth to put action to my faith and when I did, there was no back pain!

I started this particular morning with exercise and ended it by carrying bags of groceries. All pain is gone! Praise the Lord, I am healed!

J. M.

Florence, South Carolina

Heart Restored

In 1974 I had a heart attack and have had open heart surgery since that time. I was scheduled for a triple bypass; however, when the doctors were performing the surgery, they found that 25 to 40 percent of my heart had been dead for eleven years. They decided not to perform a triple bypass, so they performed a double bypass.

For the past eleven years I have visited the hospital twenty-two times, but my problem could never be corrected. I suffered with a lot of pain.

One night I was in one of your services. You told the congregation that earlier that afternoon you had a vision of God giving someone a new heart.

I came forward to receive my healing and as you prayed for me, I felt the power of God working around my heart and it felt wonderful. I didn't have any pain.

Several days later, I went to the doctor's office to be checked and he confirmed that the 25 to 40 percent of my heart that had been dead for eleven years was healthy and functioning normally. Praise God, He gave me a new heart!

D. P.

South Carolina

Back Healed

I have had a lot of back problems and pain for two years. As a result, it has been hard for me to get out of bed in the mornings.

One night I was in one of your services and you called me out to lay hands on me. I went forward and when you prayed for me, I believed I received my healing.

The next morning my healing manifested, and instead of rolling out of bed, I jumped out! I thank God He has healed me!

E. P.

South Carolina

Hip and Leg Restored

I was in a car accident when I was ten years old and because of the severity of my injuries, the doctors didn't expect me to live. The trauma my body experienced caused me to go into a coma, which resulted in my body curling up into a fetal position.

Regardless of the circumstances, my parents believed God for me to live. The doctors told them that if I did live, I would be a vegetable.

When I came out of the coma, I had brain damage and had to learn how to walk, talk, and eat again. Even though I regained the ability to perform these functions, I was left with damage to my hip and leg.

I was at one of your services, and you called me out to pray for me. As you did, I felt a warm sensation hit my hip and spread down my leg.

After several years of pain and surgeries, I am now completely healed! Praise God!

H. M.
Indiana

Stomach Lump Healed

For a year and a half, I had a lump in my stomach that measured about four or five inches.

I was attending one of your meetings and as you were ministering to a woman, you cursed lumps. I was sitting in my seat and I felt the power of God working in my lower stomach area.

I went to the ladies' room to check the lump that I had in my stomach and it was shrinking! Praise God, I am healed!

L. T.
Massachusetts

Double Healing

I had a lump in my breast and problems with my right hip for some time.

During one of your services that I attended, you called out for those who had lumps in their bodies to come forward so you could pray for them.

While you were praying for those who went forward, my lump disappeared.

You also prayed for someone who had a hip problem, and while you were praying for them, my hip was healed as well.

Praise God! I am healed!

L. L.
Massachusetts

Spine and Knee Healed

When I was in the fourth grade, I tore some ligaments in my left knee. As a result there were many times my kneecap would pop out of place.

The only thing that could correct this problem was to have surgery. However, even after the surgery it was never the same. I always had problems with it and catered to that knee when I walked to avoid pain.

During one of your services, you called me out and prayed for me. I felt the power of God on my knee. I began to do deep knee bends with no pain!

My spine was also crooked and my girlfriend actually felt it straighten. I'm healed!

T. G.
Indiana

268

God's Word Is Best Medicine

I have been suffering from a chemical dependency on nerve medication for ten years. My dependency on the medication was so great that I did not dare go anywhere without my medication being at arm's reach.

At one time, the doctors attempted to wean me off the medication and I became totally helpless and almost succeeded at a suicide attempt.

I attended one of your meetings and while you were preaching the Word, I began to soak up every scripture and word you were saying. In the past, the medication never allowed me to concentrate and retain what I heard.

You called out my healing and I felt a peace come over me. I felt *free!*

I am now functioning normally with greater peace than I have ever felt in all my life! I am drug free and my nerve medication is now **God's Word!**

D. B.

Ohio

No More Traction

For two years I had suffered with extreme pain in my neck and shoulders which left me with no use of my right shoulder and arm. I used a home traction machine two hours daily to alleviate the pain.

You called me out during a service and prayed for me. I felt a warm sensation start in my neck and then spread over my shoulder and down my arm.

The following day, I had no pain! I didn't need to take any pain medication and I didn't need to use my home traction machine.

I was healed! I can now raise my right hand straight up and I am improving daily.

J. C.

West Virginia

Child's Deformed Feet Healed

My husband and I had been praying and believing God for our daughter's healing. She was born with deformed feet which resulted in her inability to walk. Both of her feet were turned out and her ankles leaned in. She had to have a cotton arch placed in each of her shoes to help pull her feet inward, which was very uncomfortable for her.

During your meeting, you called for those who needed prayer. I had felt a strong urge in my spirit that you should lay hands on her, so I went and got her from the nursery and brought her into the healing line.

When you came to us, you took her in your arms and set her on your lap, holding both of her feet in your hands as you prayed. After you prayed, you told her to start walking and as she started to walk, both of her feet were made perfectly straight and her ankles no longer lean inward! She walked perfectly and ran for the very *first time* in her life! Praise the Lord!

C. R.

Massachusetts

Spine Pops Into Place

I had been afflicted for fifteen years with several physical problems. I suffered with curvature of the spine, arthritis, and sinus and allergy problems.

Because of the problem with my spine, I couldn't move my arm very easy which made it hard to do some of the basic things.

I attended one of your meetings and you laid your hands on me and commanded the spirit of infirmity to leave. When you did that, my spine started popping into place. I raised my arm straight above my head and moved my neck around freely which I wasn't able to do before.

At 3:00 a.m. the next morning I woke up praising God. Hallelujah! Jesus is the Healer!

K. M.

Alabama

No Longer Needs Thirty Medications

I suffered with Crohn's disease for two years. During this time I was on twenty-five to thirty different medications, none of which helped me to stop shaking.

By this time, I had quit my second job and I was afraid of everything. I had become a prisoner of my own home. My pastor called and told me that you were coming to our church. I became very excited. I dug out all of your tapes that I'd had for years and listened to them daily. I had not been to church for fear of "shaking" other people's faith. What a lie! I felt like

271

the woman trying to touch the hem of Jesus' garment. It was destined for me to be in those meetings.

As you ministered to me, I was totally delivered from Crohn's disease and from the spirit of fear. Before my healing I battled fifty symptoms a day.

My doctor took me off of all the medications because they made me sick. I will never receive the spirit of fear again. Praise God, I'm healed and this was a "piece of cake" for Him!

B. M.
Michigan

God Is a Restorer

When you prayed for me back in 1987, I had just lost twins. The doctors told me that I wasn't supposed to have a baby, but you said I would have a baby.

I had a lot of problems carrying my daughter to full term, but I continued to remember the prophecy that you spoke over me.

I think you should know when something great comes from your prophecies — our daughter!

C. H.
Bay City, Michigan

Hips Healed

I slipped and fell about two years ago. I didn't go to any doctor. I had developed a limp and my hips had hurt ever since I had fallen.

The day after hearing you in a service, I walked out of a store and noticed a strange feeling. I told my daughter Shirley, "Hey, I'm healed!" The limp and pain in my hips were all gone. Praise God!

M. L.

Morristown, Tennessee

Knot Disappears

A small knot had been on the back of my neck for five months. You said, "Everyone who has knots on them, stand up." So I stood up.

You asked me where the knot was. I put my hand on the place where the knot was, but the knot was gone. Hallelujah! I was healed!

V. R.

Morristown, Tennessee

New Heart Received

I attended one of your services. During the service, you prayed for people.

I received a new heart at seventy-five years old and it is working great!

Thanks for praying for new hearts. It was my time!

D. M.

Blood Condition Healed

Recently you were ministering here in Florida. During the latter part of the service you were ministering to individuals in the congregation.

You laid hands on me and said I was being healed of a blood condition. Hallelujah! I have been healed!

R. W.

Epilepsy Healed

My son has had epilepsy for a little over a year. We took him to a pediatric neurologist for medical treatment for epilepsy at least once a week.

My son started having seizures when he was a year and a half old. The seizures were so bad that he would stop breathing. Every time he would get sick, he would have a seizure and he was sick all the time.

You came to minister in our church and I attended the service. When the Spirit of God fell in that place, I knew that my son would be healed. I took him up front and you laid hands on him. I knew he was healed.

One month later I took my son to Geisinger to have another EEG. The first EEG showed that he had irregular brain waves. The EEG after you laid hands on him came back normal. We now only have to go to Geisinger once every six months.

My son now has color back in his face and no longer looks sickly. I thank God for his healing.

T. S.

New Ovary Received

For two years I have had severe problems with menstruation. During that time I would have such severe pain that I went to the emergency room on several occasions. The doctors ran multiple tests on me, but they could not find anything wrong, yet I continued to get worse.

At one point, I bled every day for three months. A minister prayed for me during that time and the bleeding stopped, but the pain did not. All the doctors could do was to prescribe strong pain medication. I had been on high doses of several narcotic painkillers.

I attended another meeting you had in Colorado. In one of the evening services, you said there was an angel there with a new ovary for someone.

To be honest with you, I wasn't sure if that was for me, because I didn't know if I needed a new ovary. But when you said that, I felt a hot oil come all over me and penetrate that particular area.

I was out for maybe a split second and then I came to. I knew after the service that I would never have trouble with my menstrual cycle again.

Right after that meeting, on my way back to Tulsa, I started my menstrual cycle. At first I started to take some medicine just out of habit, but then I realized after a few hours that I had not had any pain. I ended up going through my whole menstrual cycle without any pain or discomfort. It was a miracle from God!

I was so blessed by your ministry. Thank you for obeying God!

J. S.

Back Disc Healed

We have really been blessed by the Lord through your ministry. The first time I saw you, the Lord healed me of lower back disc problems. You had laid hands on me at our church in California.

Night before last, you laid hands on my wife for a thyroid problem that the devil thought he was going to make permanent. Praise God, we have victory in Jesus!

M. B.
Murrieta, California

Wedding Bells

I was introduced to your ministry in Virginia, and I asked you to pray that God would give me a husband. You did and God gave me my husband. We have been married since 1996 and we love each other very much.

I just want to thank you and your ministry for your prayers and your love.

L. S.
Illinois

Hearing Restored

In April 1998, I lost all hearing in my left ear during our rehearsal for the Easter musical.

My head felt stuffed up and began to ring all the time. It became very painful to be in a noisy area.

Several visits to the hearing specialist showed no physical reason for the hearing loss.

I stood on God's Word that my sickness had been taken away by the blood of Jesus.

During this time, you ministered at our church. During the service you called out that God was healing someone's left ear and reconstructing it.

Immediately, I claimed that healing for myself. Within a short time, *all* hearing was restored. All symptoms left. I praise God for total healing!

D. S.

Longmont, Colorado

Breast Lump Healed

About thirteen years ago you came to our church with another minister. During the service you called out someone with a lump in their breast, so I went forward.

When you laid your hands on my forehead, a honey-like feeling flowed over my body. When it hit my breast it was like a "pins and needles" feeling. When I finally came to, the lump was totally gone and it never returned. Glory to God!

K. B.

Longmont, Colorado

Bad Heart Valve Healed

In early 1984 I attended a Ministers' Conference in Arkansas. You were one of the speakers during an evening session. You called me out from the audience. Through a word of knowledge, you told me I had a bad valve in my heart from rheumatic fever as a child.

When I went forward I began to feel a warmth all over me. I fell backwards with no one behind me. As I laid on the floor, I could feel an angel touching my heart. I looked up and there were ten big angels around you.

You said to me, "Do you know you have an angel doing surgery on your heart?" I said, "Yes, I can feel it."

As a result of this experience, I have a new heart! Just one time after that did I experience a "heart flutter," but I rebuked it and it has never returned.

M.H.
Colorado Springs, Colorado

Lumps Healed

I had three lumps in my breast (possibly cancer). After Dr. Dufresne prayed for me, two of the lumps completely disappeared and one shrank and became normal.

W. A.
Boalsburg, PA

Tumors Disappear

I attended one of your services. During the service, you called for those to come forward who had lumps or bumps, and as my wife was going forward, you called out that there was a tumor the size of a tangerine. She had fibroid tumors in her breast, one being the size of a tangerine.

Today she got a report from the doctors after having some tests done to confirm that the tumors are no longer there!

She went into the doctor's office and he said that maybe the hormone pills he prescribed had worked. She said, "No," since she had only taken two, but she said she had received prayer and that's why the tumors disappeared.

J. A.

Tulsa, Oklahoma

Heart Condition Healed

I was healed of a heart condition and it's still holding good. I was healed while sitting in the congregation when the Lord was moving by His Spirit and you called me up to the platform to testify. When you prayed for me, my 230 pound body fell upon you and you were pinned underneath me. Remember?

Brother, it was worth it all! Glory to God!

B. T.

Riverside, California

A Family Grows

I have seen you preach many times and you are my favorite guest speaker that we've had. My husband and I had been believing God for children for almost three years when you came to our church and had a prayer line for women who wanted to get pregnant.

I went up for prayer and within that same month, I got pregnant and then again the next year.

Thank you! My boys are wonderful!

B. H.
Knoxville, Tennessee

Part V
To My Husband

To My Husband

This book was written in obedience to the Spirit of God, to bring glory to God, and to bless the body of Christ. But it's also a cherished way for me to honor you, my husband, a precious man of God.

Ed, you are the man of my dreams, the husband heaven has ordained for me to be joined to, a precious treasure in my life, and a priceless gift to the body of Christ.

Thank you for loving me. Thank you for the joy you are in my life. Thank you for helping me to know my heavenly Father better.

With unending love,

Nancy

Other Books

by Dr. Ed Dufresne

Faithfulness: The Road To Divine Promotion
Praying God's Word
There's A Healer In The House
Anointings & Mantels
The Prophet: Friend of God
Faith That Makes A Demand On The Anointing
Devil, Don't Touch My Stuff!
Fresh Oil From Heaven

Other Books

by Nancy Dufresne

Daily Healing Bread From God's Table
His Presence Shall Be My Dwelling Place
Victory In The Name
The Healer Divine